FRANCIS

FRANCIS
A CALL TO CONVERSION

• • • • • • • • • • • • • •

DUANE W.H. ARNOLD
C. GEORGE FRY

Foreword by
JOHN MICHAEL TALBOT, OSF

CANTILEVER BOOKS
Zondervan Publishing House
Grand Rapids, Michigan

Cantilever Books is an imprint of Zondervan Publishing House, 1415 Lake Drive S.E., Grand Rapids, Michigan 49506.

Edited by Michael G. Smith
Designed by James E. Ruark

Library of Congress Cataloging in Publication Data

Arnold, Duane W. H.
    Francis : a call to conversion / Duane W. H. Arnold and C. George Fry ; foreword by John Michael Talbot.
    p.   cm.
    Bibliography: p.
    Includes index.
    ISBN 0-310-52060-6
    1. Francis, of Assisi, Saint, 1182–1226. 2. Christian saints—Italy—Assisi—Biography. 3. Assisi (Italy)—Biography. I. Fry, C. George. II. Title.
BX4700.F6A79   1988
271'.3'024—dc19   88-28122
[B]   CIP

Printed in the United States of America
88 89 90 91 92 93 / BC / 10 9 8 7 6 5 4 3 2 1

To
Terry Waite

"Blessed are the peacemakers"

Contents

Foreword

Francis of Assisi! His name is familiar to nearly all the Christians of the world. Yet Francis' name, not far behind the name of Jesus, has often been obscured in a cloud of confusion by those well-meaning seekers after God who have sought to justify their own religious opinions by appealing to his example.

Francis of Assisi was a man whose vision was clear and whose example was uncompromising, yet he ever remains a paradox of faith to us all. He was a stalwart follower of Christ, yet he is esteemed as a holy man by those of many other religions. He was an obedient son of the Roman Catholic Church, yet he is held up high as a mirror of gospel perfection by those of all Christian persuasions. He is looked upon as the founder of the many religious orders of men and women who have institutionally constituted the Franciscan Family over the last 800 years; yet Francis himself continually confounds all attempts to overly structure or institutionalize the gift which was given to him to radically and simply "live the Gospel."

It is the universal appeal of Francis of Assisi which the authors of this book have tried to capture and describe for Catholics and Protestants alike. It is ironic that Francis, who was fervent in his obedience to the Roman Catholic Church, has been looked upon by both Protestant and Catholic reformers as a primary inspiration to return to the pure roots of the Gospel of Christ from which the early apostolic church first received the strength to grow and flower. It is true that Francis shared this "apostolic" sense of faith with them in his radical call to live the Gospel. Consequently, many who have sought to

return to the purity of the early apostolic and truly catholic church of
the New Testament have found in Francis of Assisi an example, a
prophet, and a friend.

Today's writers, I assume, will be no exception to history. As
modern reformers, the authors of this book see in Francis an inspiring
example of apostolic purity and universal catholicity which is so direly
needed and desired in the church today.

In this book the authors cover dimensions of Francis' life and
spirituality from a number of unique perspectives. Rooted deeply in
Scripture and the apostolic tradition of the early church, they see
Francis of Assisi as having much in common with the later Protestant
reformers and movements. Remaining true to their position as
"evangelical catholics," the authors have skillfully and honestly put
together a presentation of Francis that reaches deep into the heart of
Christians of many varying points of view. Yet the vision of the book
calls all Christians forward in the work of reuniting the broken body of
Christ and redeeming the societies in which we live—tasks which ever
remain primary concerns for every man, woman, and child who
honestly seek to call themselves Christians.

As both a Roman Catholic and a Franciscan, I am deeply
touched by this present work, which these, my brothers and friends,
have so lovingly brought forth. I must confess my fear that they might
have but added their names, along with mine, to the long list of those
who have tried to describe the enigma of Francis' simple faith in the
weighted words of systematic Christian thought. Yet this attempt is
not at all in vain. We who are so profoundly and deeply inspired by the
awesome work of the Spirit among our brothers and sisters in this
world often need the objective means of written discourse by which we
can begin to grasp this "mystical wind" of God.

Through my long association with the authors, I am firmly
convinced that they write from the same inner fire of God that has
burned within so many others who have written about Francis over the
last eight centuries. This, I think, is of primary importance; for in the
long run, it remains Francis' fire, not his logic, which inspires so many
in our world to follow his example of the Gospel without compromise.
It is my prayer that this book will aid in calling all its readers to
precisely that end.

We live in a world facing monumental problems of political
injustice, poverty, and the continuing threat of a nuclear holocaust.

These are the days for Christians to unite in the radical call of Christ which so strongly burned within the heart of Francis of Assisi.

So read this book with an open mind and perhaps Francis will open your heart. In an attitude of sharing, rather than argumentation, Protestant brothers and sisters might well find themselves becoming more understanding of Catholics, and Catholic brothers and sisters might well find themselves becoming more understanding of Protestants. It is then, when we embrace one another in the "holy fire" of the Gospel that we will find our hearts eternally melted together in the power of the love of God. It is then that we may truly call ourselves brothers and sisters in our Lord Jesus Christ. It is then that we may more truly understand the vision of Francis of Assisi.

JOHN MICHAEL TALBOT, OSF
The Little Portion
Eureka Springs, Arkansas

Acknowledgments

The authors would like to thank those whose encouragement, advice and assistance aided the research, writing, and publishing of this book. Many persons have influenced our understanding of Francis; far too many to mention in this brief space. Some, however, have shared so generously of their time and expertise that we would be remiss not to name them. We owe a debt to those scholars who graciously read and commented upon the manuscript, especially Professor James Atkinson, the University of Sheffield; the Rt. Rev. John R. H. Moorman, sometime Lord Bishop of Ripon; and the late Professor Harold J. Grimm, the Ohio State University, whose death has denied us the opportunity to share with him the final results of this project which he so encouraged.

In a special category is our longtime friend and companion in pilgrimage Brother John Michael Talbot, OSF, who has provided not only consolation on the way, but the kind remarks and reflections contained in the foreword to this book.

There are others who have been supporting persons in the communities in which we have lived and worked while preparing the text. Especially we would thank the principal, fellows, tutors, and members of Saint Chad's College, the University of Durham, and the religious community of Saint Francis College, Fort Wayne, Indiana, particularly Sister M. JoEllen Scheetz, president.

A disclaimer, of course, is in order. Errors in fact or interpretation are the responsibility of the authors alone. With the venerable church historian, Eusebius of Caesarea, we can only say, "I trust that kindly disposed readers will pardon the deficiencies of the work, for I confess that my powers are inadequate to do full justice to so ambitious an undertaking" (*Church History*, I, 1).

We would be negligent if we failed to give due recognition to the efforts of our editor, Michael G. Smith, who lovingly watched over the "mysterious process" by which a manuscript becomes a book and thereby gained the authors' respect and thanks.

Finally, as we write these acknowledgments, one man remains foremost in our hearts and minds. Few in our time better embody the ideals of Francis than Anglican envoy Terry Waite. Although unseen and silent for many months, Terry Waite has remained an eloquent symbol of the Franciscan calling to be a peacemaker. It is to him that this book is dedicated.

DUANE W. H. ARNOLD   C. GEORGE FRY
Wayne State University   St. Francis College
Detroit, Michigan   Fort Wayne, Indiana

Ash Wednesday 1988

Introduction

We must refer every good to the most high supreme God, acknowledging that all good belongs to him; and we must thank him for it all, because all good comes from him. May the most supreme and high and only true God receive and have and be paid all honour and reverence, all praise and blessing, all thanks and all glory, for to him belongs all good and "no one is good but only God."[1]

Jesus said, "I, if I be lifted up from the earth, will draw all men unto me" (John 12:32). Already in the first generation of Christianity this prophecy was fulfilled. All manner of persons were drawn to Christ. Among those earliest believers three names are prominent.

Firstly, there was Peter, the apostle of order. Called "the rock," he was the administrator and the organizer of the early community. From Jerusalem to Rome, Peter was recognized as the preeminent personality of primitive Christianity. His legacy to the church has been interpreted by subsequent generations as that of catholicism. His was a comprehensive sense of what it meant to be a Christian. It was he who spoke of a "priesthood" of all believers. It was he who encouraged the suffering believers in the regions of Asia Minor. It was he who called on Christians to "offer up spiritual sacrifices, acceptable to God by Jesus Christ" (1 Peter 2:5). It was he who compared the Church to a new Temple, "a spiritual house." It was he who wrote of Jesus as the "Shepherd and Bishop" of our souls. It was he who as an "elder" encouraged other "elders" to fulfill their offices with grace and humility. And it was he who advised Christians to "have fervent charity among yourselves." Catholic Christians of all centuries have seen in Peter their father and founder.

Secondly, there was Paul, the apostle of candor. Called "the Doctor of the Gentiles," Paul was the confessor and theologian of early Christianity. From Jerusalem to Rome, Paul taught the faithful and witnessed to those without. His legacy to the church has been interpreted by subsequent generations as that of evangelicalism. His was a faith of confession and proclamation. It was he who wrote of "the righteousness of God revealed from faith to faith; as it is written, the just shall live by their faith" (Rom. 1:17). It was he who instructed believers to "know that all things work together for good for those who love God, to those who are called according to his purpose" (Rom. 8:28). It was he who assured Christians that "there is therefore now no condemnation for those who are in Christ Jesus" (Rom 8:1). It was Paul who laid the groundwork for the great doctrines of Law and Grace, later expostulated by Augustine, and still later, by Luther and Calvin. Classical Protestantism drew heavily on Pauline thought in its theology. Evangelical Christians of all centuries have seen in Paul their mentor and model.

Finally, there was John, the apostle of ardor. Called "the beloved disciple," John was known, loved, and respected as a living embodiment of the spirit of Jesus. A person of passion, he had in his ministry an apocalyptic urgency that tradition tells us spanned the miles from Jerusalem to Patmos. Filled with a sense of destiny, John brought to believers a burning vision of the ascended Christ. Radical in his commitment to love and justice, he was described as "your brother in tribulation, and in the kingdom and patience of Jesus Christ" (Rev. 1:9). In the Johannine tradition, this one who could prophesy the fall of empires was the very same person who admonished the faithful, "beloved, let us love one another; for love is of God" (1 John 4:7). It was this tradition that emphasized the righteousness of nations and the holiness of persons committed to Christ, "for this is the love of God, that we keep his commandments" (1 John 5:3). It was this John who knew the reality of Christian affection and the world's affliction. It is this John who has been the inspiring figure for dissenters and seers of subsequent centuries. Radical Christians of many persuasions are honored to own his name and fulfill his calling.

Since the age of the apostles these three traditions—the Catholic, the Evangelical, and the Radical—have coexisted within World Christianity. To some extent most Christian bodies retain elements of each heritage, as to some extent all Christians find within themselves ingredients of the Petrine, the Pauline, and the Johannine perspectives. The problem, however, is that it has been extremely difficult for any institution or any individual to comprehend fully the totality of Christ to which these traditions witness. Already in the first century Peter and Paul were at odds and some regarded the Johannine vision as suspect. In subsequent church history there has often been polarization. Mutual misunderstanding and distrust have arisen. The catholicism of a Cyprian, an Aquinas, or a Loyola has been hard to reconcile with the evangelicalism of an Augustine, a Luther, or a Calvin, and these likewise have difficulty comprehending the radicalism of a Tertullian, an Arndt, a Bunyan, or a Fox. As Christians, however, we have had "committed unto us the word of reconciliation" (2 Cor. 5:19). There has been a call to redeem our realities in church and society alike.

Francis of Assisi stands within this tradition of mediation and redemption. A son of the church catholic, Francis was a man of evangelical principles called to a mission of radical renewal. Francis was a man of catholic fellowship, evangelical faith, and radical freedom. These traits have commended him to Christians of all these persuasions. Francis would be comfortable with a Thomas More, a Philip Melanchthon, or a Menno Simons. Thomas More, a Catholic martyr of the English Reformation, was in fact a Third Order Franciscan. Philip Melanchthon, author of the Augsburg Confession, a classic statement of evangelicalism, praised Francis as "a holy father" and extolled him as a precursor of the Reformation ideal. Menno Simons, beloved leader of the Radical Reformation, championed and popularized the Franciscan virtues of simplicity, peace, and service. The influence of Francis is almost universal within the Christian family.

Francis is found everywhere. In the city of London a private collector possesses a work by Rembrandt entitled "St. Francis." This is an unusual portrait, as it is one of the few known Rembrandt portrayals of a nonbiblical saint. In the painting Francis holds a crucifix in one hand while an open Bible lies before him. The artist recognized Francis as a reconciler, for Rembrandt, himself a dissenter, showed Francis embracing the symbols of both Catholicism and evangelicalism.

Francis is found everywhere. Some years ago one of the authors was driving through Dayton, Ohio. In the distance he saw an inviting church tower. Obeying an internal summons, he turned in the direction of the sanctuary. Arriving at the impressive structure, he saw beside it a garden in which there was a statue of Francis of Assisi. He assumed that this must be a Roman Catholic church. To his surprise, the name of the church on the bulletin board read "Shiloh Congregational Church."

Francis is found everywhere. The other author, living in England, stopped by a small, ruined monastic chapel and inquired of the groundskeeper as to what had taken place. The keeper was a local historian, who was able to tell him the whole story. It was related that the church had been destroyed in the seventeenth century during the English Civil War by the followers of Oliver Cromwell. The author was told that every statue had been pulled down and thrown into a nearby pond. That is, every statue save one—that of Francis of Assisi. The Lord Protector's followers had spared it, recognizing in Francis a kindred heart.

Francis' ministry of reconciliation and redemption has never been so needed as today. The twentieth century has witnessed something of a revival of World Christianity. Catholicism continues to grow and to make a significant impact on society. Evangelicalism has come to the forefront in North America in the past generation while it expands dramatically in the Third World. Radicalism, as a need to return to New Testament norms of love and justice, commends itself to many. One need only glance at the periodical shelves of any major seminary or university library to realize the vitality of these three traditions. *America* and *Commonweal, Christianity Today* and *Eternity, Weavings* and *The Church Times, Sojourners* and *The Other Side* all command significant readerships and exercise vast influence.

A note of caution must be sounded, however. These movements of renewal could further divide an already fractured Christian community. They challenge us to take up the Franciscan ministry of mediation and interpretation. We must redeem our realities. If we fail in this mission of reconciliation, our age may see yet further polarization in the Christian churches. The need of the day is for "an instrument of peace" to draw together catholic, evangelical, and radical Christians.

The purpose of this book is to present once more the story of Francis of Assisi, but to do so in light of the needs of the Christian community in the late twentieth century. Viewing Francis as a minister of reconciliation requires many things. The book begins biographically, placing Francis within the context of his times. This is, indeed, difficult, for Francis, like one of his followers, is "a man for all seasons." The subsequent section explores his abiding relevance for Christians of all traditions. Each of the chapters in this section is drawn out of his life and ministry and examines his significance for the major issues that both confront and divide the church today: worship, theology, society, and destiny. We conclude with a bibliographical essay indicating some of the formative evangelical, catholic, and radical influences on the authors of this present study.

Philip Schaff, esteemed Swiss-American church historian, once observed that Peter represented the tradition of hope, Paul that of faith, and John that of love. To us it is imperative that the Christians of today come to terms with the issues of belonging, believing, and becoming. As we take up this task of being God's people in a new age and, indeed, redeeming our realities, we are aided in the process of evaluating our common roots—catholic, evangelical, and radical—by the model provided by Francis of Assisi.

One

Life

... Sent From God

"There was a man sent from God, whose name was John."

There was a man sent from God, whose name was John" (John 1:6). How often these words have been spoken in a spirit of gratitude within the church of Jesus Christ.

"There was a man sent from God, whose name was John." These words are first stated at the beginning of the New Testament. Initially they refer to St. John the Baptist, cousin of Jesus, last of the Old Testament prophets, first of the New Testament preachers, herald of Christ. This John came as a fulfillment of prophecy, for Malachi, whose book closes the Old Testament canon, reported the word of God: "Behold I will send my messenger, and he shall prepare the way before me . . . " (Mal. 3:1; Mark 1:2). Christ's covenant is announced by one who "did baptize in the wilderness, and preach the baptism of repentance for the remission of sins" (Mark 1:4). In the earliest Gospel, that of Mark, containing the preaching of St. Peter in Rome, the first portrait offered is that of a man "whose name was John."

"There was a man sent from God, whose name was John." The New Testament opens with the voice of St. John the Baptist; it closes with the vision of St. John the Divine. Exiled to the Isle of Patmos, possibly working in the salt mines, the John of the Apocalypse, like the

23

John of the Wilderness, preached Christ, writing, "I was in the Spirit on the Lord's day, and heard behind me a great voice, as of a trumpet, saying, 'I am the Alpha and Omega, the first and the last . . . " (Rev. 1:10–11). As it began, so the New Testament record ends, with a man, whose name was John, proclaiming an imminent Christ.

"There was a man sent from God, whose name was John." This promise was realized in the early ministry of Jesus. John was among the first called by Christ to be an apostle, summoned along with his brother James and Simon Peter (Luke 5:10). This John became "the disciple . . . whom he loved" (John 19:26), to whom the Master said, referring to Mary, "Behold your mother" (John 19:27). To him was given the privilege of having the Virgin Mother come "unto his own home" (John 19:27). From earliest times this John has been immortalized in the iconography of the church, for he is represented standing, along with Mary, at the foot of the cross. The Johannine literature, both Gospel and Epistles, further commemorates his place in the Christian tradition.

"There was a man sent from God, whose name was John." Among the many illustrious men to bear the name of the preacher, the seer, and the disciple in the subsequent history of the church is one who defies all classifications of geography and history. By birth he is a member of the Church of the South, Italian in origin, whose ministry was realized within the context of the Latin church. By influence he is a citizen of all Christendom. In the East, to the Orthodox, this John is esteemed a saint, revered as a living icon, an embodiment of the Jesus Prayer. In the North, in the world of Lutheranism and Calvinism, this John is, according to an evangelical confession of the Reformation, a "father" of the church who believed himself "justified by faith."[1] In the West, to the Anglican and Free churches, he is sage and seer, prophet and poet.

A Christian may encounter the hymns of this John being sung at Presbyterian Communion services, Anglican ordinations, or Baptist meetings. One may see his statue in both Catholic and Congregationalist churchyards. This John is mentor both to evangelicals and Anglo-Catholics. Surely this man, baptized as "John, son of Peter Bernardone," but known to us as Francis of Assisi, was sent from God. His life has a significance that transcends the normal limitations of history and geography, for Francis is not merely a child of the Italian Middle Ages, but is very much a universal man—a person of the twenty-first century.

Early Life, 1181–1204

John, or Giovanni de Pietro de Bernardone, later named Francis after his mother's homeland, was born in the Italian town of Assisi, nestled in the austere hills of Umbria. We are uncertain as to the exact date of his birth. Probably it was the year 1181, although some maintain it was 1182. Some say it was summer, others insist it was the autumn when the first child of Pietro and Pica de Bernardone came into the world. It has been said that the hour of our birth is a revelation of the years of our lives. Certainly this was true of many of the characters of the biblical narrative, like Samuel, Moses, Isaac, and St. John the Baptist. This also seems to have been true of Francis. His early biographers point out at least four "signs" or important marks surrounding his birth which were to be prophetic of his subsequent career.

The first was his baptismal name, John. The earliest biographers were impressed with this coincidence. The name Giovanni was apparently bestowed upon him by his mother to honor St. John the Baptist. Due to this connection, many comparisons between the ministries of Francis and the Prophet of the Wilderness would be made by later Franciscans. One of these, Thomas of Celano, the earliest of the biographers of Francis, wrote:

> The name John referred to the work of the ministry which he would undertake. The name Francis referred to the spread of his fame, which after he had been fully converted to God, quickly

spread everywhere. He considered the feast of John the Baptist to be more illustrious than the feasts of all the other saints, for the dignity of his name left a mark of mystic virtue upon him.[2]

The second "prophetic sign" was the person of his mother, Mona Pica. In Franciscan tradition the mother of Francis was always thought of as "an excellent woman, and like another Elizabeth."[3] Several of the writers, knowing his father's reputation for harshness, felt that Francis had received his gentleness and grace from his French-born mother. It was probably she who engendered in Francis his great love of poetry. To the very end of his life Francis would remember with joy the French songs and verses taught to him by his mother. Being the daughter of a French knight of Provence, Pica appears to have also related to her child the ideals of chivalry. Later Francis would think of himself as "a knight of Christ" who, in loving obligation, served his "Lady Poverty."

There is also the paradoxical figure of his father Pietro. The earliest biographers of Francis may well have been impressed with this other coincidence of names. While they might have wished to compare his father Pietro to the Peter of Scripture, "the Prince of the Apostles," they must have quickly concluded that contrasts were more in keeping with the character of the two men. Pietro was a merchant of cloth, not a fisher of men. He traveled for profit, not to proclaim the faith. He sought his fortune in this world, not the next. He was, however, similar to Peter in that he was a rash and emotional man, quick to anger. What Pietro's emotions would have been at the birth of his first son we do not know, for he was absent on a business journey. His physical separation at the boy's birth would be matched by a spiritual alienation throughout his son's life.

Fathers and sons sometimes are unable or unwilling to reciprocate love. As church historians we are reminded of the great psychological distance that separated Martin Luther from his father Hans. Although this case has been much examined and at times exaggerated, the fact of the filial separation remains.[4] The similarities between the fathers of Luther and Francis are indeed striking. Hans Luther and Pietro de Bernardone were both striving businessmen, social climbers, and seekers of wealth. Both profoundly misunderstood their sons and virulently opposed their religious vocations. Both could not comprehend why a child, nurtured in affluence and destined for secular success, would reject middle-class security and morality for the alternative lifestyle of poverty and celibacy. This meant that both

Francis and Luther, when they took their vows of obedience to their heavenly Father, were simultaneously engaging in acts of disobedience to their earthly fathers. This seems an indication of their future vocations to be "obedient rebels."

The last "sign" concerned Francis' baptism. Often in Scripture and tradition, at the time of "naming" there comes a mysterious stranger who foretells the fame of the child. Tradition ascribes this to the infancy of Francis. As Wise Men brought regal gifts and visited baby Jesus, so on the day of the baptism of Francis "a pilgrim stopped to beg at the door." He was a mendicant, pledged to poverty, who implored, "I beg you to show me the child born today for I greatly wish to see him." The maid, who had opened the door to him, drew back in fear at this eloquent and urgent embodiment of poverty. She insisted that it was impossible for him to come near to the child,

> but, when the Lady Pica heard what had happened, she was amazed and told the maid to show the child to the stranger. When this was done, the pilgrim took the baby into his arms with great devotion and joy, as Simeon had once taken the infant Jesus.[5]

This foretold Francis' future life as "the Little Poor One" who would literally fulfill the injunction of Jesus to the rich young man to "sell all that you have, and distribute to the poor, and you shall have treasure in heaven: and come, follow me" (Luke 18:22).

Although these signs illumine the infancy of Francis as a star cast light on the nativity of Jesus, the childhood of the saint, like that of the Savior, is shrouded in obscurity. Occasionally there are glimpses of the lad as he comes of age, but these are often contradictory. It is said that he seldom attended the school of St. George in Assisi, yet the boy knew a little Latin, more French, and was eloquent in his native medieval Italian. Stories are told of his buffoonery, though as a young man he already espoused the code of chivalry. Sickly and often ill, he nevertheless enjoyed nothing more than "soldiering" with his teenage cohorts in the countryside, as beneath the pines of Umbria they enacted Crusader scenes set beneath the palms of Palestine. Although not fond of the sagas of the church, Francis and his friends were enamored by the tales of the troubadours such as the *Song of Roland*.

Francis was not a handsome man. His features were undistinguished. As he was the eldest, however, it is reported that his father's ambitions centered around him, causing the other children born to Mona Pica to be largely ignored and forgotten. Although we know little of his siblings, it was common knowledge in the town that his father aspired to see Francis marry into the ranks of the lesser Italian nobility. Francis was sometimes said to be shy and retiring; nevertheless, he was recognized as the leader of the young men of the town, especially in acts of rebellion, for in him many of them found their model and their master.

These conflicting vignettes simply confirm the fact that Francis had not yet "come to himself." Part of him desired the admiration of his father and wanted to pursue the path prescribed for him. Another part of him espoused rebellion, seeking the rejection of all that his family represented. The abiding impression is that of a young man caught in a mesh of conventions and conflicting aspirations, unable to free himself because as yet he had no certain resolution as to his identity or vocation.

The Age

The inconsistencies of Francis' youthful personality matched perfectly the contradictory signs of his society. Europe was on the verge of the Renaissance, said by many an historian to be the adolescence of Western civilization. What we have is a culture caught between identities. Europe was in transition, with the old in a state of decomposition, the new not fully capable of recognition. Confusion was epidemic because few could interpret the signs of the times.

For example, there was an expansion of Christendom as Poland, Scandinavia, Hungary, and Spain were added to the Catholic family. Yet there was also a contraction of the West as repeated efforts to regain the Holy Land resulted in multiplied disasters. There had come a sense of security as feudalism flourished, solving the anarchy of the Dark Ages. In the same period, however, there was a longing for new liberties as communes and cantons rose in rebellion against their liege lords. A vision of Europe as Christendom, a holy kingdom presided over by pope and emperor was popular, but there was the reality of a continent quickly fragmenting along territorial lines into competing nations. The notion of a tripartite division of society—clergy, nobles, and peasantry, each with an allotted place and purpose in the "good society"—had come of age; yet it did not provide a place for the enigmatic and energetic middle class, committed to the ethic of capitalism, who, try as they might, could find no niche in the medieval structure.

There were signs of affluence across Europe in cathedral and guildhall, castle and monastery. There were also haunting scenes of poverty, caused by chance, not by choice, condemning millions to a marginal existence. On the one hand it was the apex of medieval civilization, symbolized by the Gothic cathedrals and the appearance of the new universities. On the other hand it was the nadir of the common culture, for the masses were illiterate, the vernacular despised; learning was for the few, not the many.

Even the saints and sages of the church seemed to be working at cross-purposes. St. Thomas Aquinas was about to compile his masterful synthesis of faith and reason, the *Summa Theologica,* long to be accepted as a normative expression of Catholicism. At the same time, the spiritual descendants of dissenter Peter Waldo continued preaching a return to the simplicity of the New Testament and apostolic era—approximating the spirit of the sixteenth-century Reformers and becoming acknowledged precursors of Protestantism.

There was a rejection of the world exhibited in a revival of monasticism. So successful was the impetus to poverty, chastity, and obedience that the pope had to forbid the formation of new orders; their proliferation had led to competition rather than cooperation in the church. During the same period, however, there was a reception of the world exhibited in a renewed lay piety. The new kind of townsman felt comfortable following Christ in the secular orders of the state, family, work, and culture. For them the godly life was that of citizen, parent, worker, and patron of the arts.

On the one hand, the pastoral office of the papacy was celebrated and extended. The pontiff now decided many matters—some theological, some political, some cultural, and some social. He was Europe's shepherd. On the other hand, the extension of papal influence was resented, resisted, and when possible, restrained by any means available. A clear line of direction was needed, but many felt that their leaders in church and state were at odds and unable to provide what was needed.

By 1199 this uncertainty expressed itself in a class war in the city of Assisi. During the previous year a thirty-eight-year-old Italian named Lotario de'Conti Segni had been elected to the chair of St. Peter in Rome and had taken the name of Innocent III. Owing to this election, the grip of the German emperor, Henry VI, on the Italian peninsula had weakened. In the city of Assisi the ancient heritage of "town liberty" had come to memory, and by the year 1202 the townsmen had sacked the ducal castle of the emperor's representative, Conrad of Swabia, forcing his retreat to the nearby town of Narni. The citizens then built a wall around the town to protect their newfound freedom from further outside aggression.

The first threat, however, came from within. Although the sacking of the ducal castle had satisfied the desires of the prominent middle class in Assisi, the poor of the city continued to go without even the basic necessities of life. Soon packs of displaced and lawless vagrants were roaming the streets until at last a civil war broke out within the walls. Internal strife, however, was soon forgotten when Assisi's neighbor to the west, Perugia, chose this moment to declare war. How much Francis was involved with the events preceding the conflict with Perugia we may only speculate, but his part in the war itself is part of the historical record.

We are told that at the opening of hostilities with Perugia, Francis and his companions were sent to battle with the blessing of the town fathers. Apparently Francis' father used this "opportunity" both to flaunt his wealth by equipping Francis for the expedition and, by his son's service, to increase his family's prestige in the community. Francis bore resplendent weapons and armor for what then ensued. In the late autumn of 1202, the finest young men of Assisi met their counterparts from Perugia on the field of battle. At Collestrada the army from Assisi was defeated, and Francis, with many others, was captured, stripped of his accouterments, and thrown into prison to await ransom.

"No One Showed Me the Way"

Francis in later years would use the words "No one showed me the way" in describing the period of his life that extended from his imprisonment at Perugia to the events surrounding his commissioning at the ruined chapel of San Damiano three years later. His time as a captive in the dungeons of Perugia was to affect his later life, both physically and spiritually. The pampered son of Bernardone was now chained hand and foot, sleeping on a filthy straw pallet. He took as his food only a minimal amount of stale bread, dried fish, and tepid water. Roughly treated by the guards, he was held only in anticipation of the money to be provided for his release.

Francis, however, reacted to the situation in a surprising way. He soon set himself apart from his companions, ceased complaining, and began singing in French the songs he had learned from his mother.

The guards initially thought that he had become mentally unstable. The other prisoners speculated that he might be trying to curry favor with his captors by his strange behavior, but they soon agreed among themselves that Bernardone's son had indeed taken leave of his senses.

Throughout the remaining time of incarceration all observed Francis. He conducted himself in an unusually polite manner, more fitted to the life of the court than the prison. He moved among the ill and the wounded, offering comfort. At length a fellow prisoner is said to have shouted at Francis, "What poor wits you once had you have certainly lost." Francis turned, replying with a smile, "You may be right, yet the time will come when the whole world will pay me homage," and then broke into song.[6]

These words are often reported in biographies of Francis. Just what did Francis mean by them? We may only guess that Bernardone's son was struggling with the dreams of his youth and the feeling that he had a great destiny, although it was still hidden and unknown to him.

Francis eventually succumbed to the conditions of prison life and for some weeks lay ill with a fever. Had his father not ransomed him, he would have certainly died in the prison of Perugia. Following his release, and in spite of the tender care of his mother, Francis failed to ever recover completely. This was but another of the seminal events of the "long year," 1204.

Conversion, 1204–1206

> . . . from that hour Francis began to consider himself as naught
> and to despise all those things he had formerly cherished; but he
> did so imperfectly, not being as yet entirely detached from worldly
> vanities. He gradually withdrew from the tumult of earthly things
> and applied himself secretly to receive Jesus Christ into his soul
> with that pearl of great price which he so desired as to be willing
> to sell all that he possessed in order to gain it.[7]

There was a man sent from God, whose name was John." God's
sending is preceded by God's calling. John the Evangelist was instantly
summoned by Jesus at the seashore. John the Baptist had the vocation
of a prophet from the very moment of his conception. This "John,"
known as Francis, however, responded to Christ's invitation only after
a prolonged process of searching and struggle. Biographers speak of six
events that transformed the "king of the feasts" into a "servant of the
poor." These events collectively constitute what we know as Francis'
conversion.

The Dream

Often in Scripture and history the life of a great man is filled with
a recurring symbol. Moses, for instance, was a man of water—being

drawn from the Nile as a child, meeting his wife by a well, crossing the Red Sea before Pharaoh's army, offending God by striking a rock to draw water from it, and finally being forbidden by the Lord to cross the river Jordan. For Jacob, there was the rock; for Joseph there was the pit. For Francis, however, there was the dream. Dreams came during critical intervals in his life. An early example of this was coupled with his second attempt to win a knight's spurs.

In the time of Francis the greatest ambition of any youth was to become a knight. The imperial law stated, "A better name than knight cannot be found for a perfect man."[8] In the spring of 1205, therefore, Francis set out as part of a campaign against the imperial barons of southern Italy. He was going to fight with the papal armies under the command of Walter de Brienne.

We know from contemporary sources that Francis was better equipped than any of the other men in his contingent, whether noblemen, squires, or footmen. The day before the warrior band was to leave Assisi, Francis encountered an impoverished knight, attired in rags, who was unable to join the expedition because he lacked the necessary equipment. Francis immediately divested himself of the arms and armor his father had given him and entrusted the poor nobleman with them.

At evening the next day, Francis found himself absorbed in thoughts of the coming campaign. Falling asleep, he had a dream. In this night vision he found himself in a splendid palace, whose walls were hung with magnificent weapons. Francis in wonderment heard a voice call out to him. Francis replied and asked who it was who owned these arms and this castle. The voice spoke and told him that these things belonged to Francis and his knights. When Francis awoke, he was convinced that the dream was an omen of great glory which was to come on the field of battle.

The company from Assisi left the following day. The end of the first leg of the journey found Francis at a hostel in Spoleto. Most scholars believe that the recurring illness of Francis, coming and going since Perugia, struck again. In his feverish half-sleep, Francis once more had a dream. A voice spoke again to him, saying, "Who do you think can best reward you, the master or the servant?"

Francis answered, "The master."

The voice responded, "Then why do you leave the master for the servant, the rich Lord for the poor man?" Francis now knew who it was that was speaking to him, and like Paul, he immediately asked, "O Lord, what do you wish me to do?"9

Francis slept no more that night. At the dawning he quickly returned to Assisi. The wisdom of the dream was confirmed by the events of history. In June 1205, the leader of the papal armies, Walter de Brienne, died in southern Italy and the expedition came to naught. For Francis, however, the dream at the hostel near Spoleto foreshadowed his career as a "Soldier of the Cross."

The Betrothal

Upon his return from Spoleto, which surprised the townspeople in Assisi, Francis resumed his place as "king of the feast." He began, however, to experience a deep depression that separated him from his fellows. His sadness alternated with moments of great exaltation, giving a sense of inconsistency to his life. Francis, for example, would frequent parties and then suddenly forsake his friends for the loneliness of the countryside. When asked to explain his conduct or to describe his cares Francis would only say that he was looking for a "treasure which was hidden." Finally, after what turned out to be his last party as the "master of the revels," his friends found an explanation of their own. Francis, they said, had fallen in love. Francis concurred.

His state was now that of a man possessed with the sweet sadness of romance. Francis declared that he would soon be betrothed to a woman of great nobility. This woman, however, was not a girl of the city or the daughter of a local signor. In fact, she was not a creature of flesh and blood. This woman was formed of mind and spirit. She reminds one of the idealized woman called "Wisdom" in Scripture, or the one named Beatrice by Dante, who afforded the poet the beatific vision. Francis named her "Lady Poverty." To Francis she came bearing gifts that were much needed—simplicity of life, clarity of purpose, and integrity of soul. She reminded Francis that "a man's life does not consist in the abundance of the things which he possesses" (Luke 12:15). Francis resolved to pledge himself to Lady Poverty. He came to love her more than life itself.

The Pilgrimage

Pilgrimage has been an important experience in the history of biblical religion. The psalter is replete with the songs sung by pilgrims as they approached Jerusalem. Christ's family made pilgrimages to the city of David, and on one occasion, child Jesus remained in the temple. Medieval Europe was obsessed with the practice of pilgrimage. Some would go so far as to cross the continent and the sea to reach the shrines of the Holy Land. Others journeyed to the great Christian sites of Europe. It is no surprise, therefore, that Francis, uncertain of his future, resolved in the year 1205 or 1206 to make a pilgrimage to the greatest shrines of European Christendom, those of Sts. Peter and Paul in Rome.

Arriving at the Old Basilica of St. Peter on Vatican Hill, Francis observed the faithful casting coins through a barred window above the bronze-covered tomb of the apostle. Most of the pious were offering paltry sums. Francis impulsively emptied his entire purse, the coins clanging on the bronze cover, while the faithful gasped. Working his way to the door of the basilica, Francis found a beggar asking alms in the atrium. Francis struck a deal with the pauper. He stripped himself of his fine clothes, gave them to the poor man, and received in return the beggar's rags. For the remainder of his stay in Rome Francis lived among the outcasts of society and knew for the first time in his life what it meant to be truly poor. It was a liberating and exhilarating experience, causing the saint of Assisi to sing aloud in French, the beloved language of his mother.

Francis wandered the streets of Rome begging alms "for the love of God." In eating the bread of necessity and taking his place in the ranks of poverty, Francis knew the truth of Christ's saying, "Happy are the poor in spirit; for theirs is the kingdom of heaven" (Matt. 5:3). This experience was his initial experiment in the life of poverty which would be his portion in the years to come.

The Kiss

The Bible is filled with moments in which a kiss is exchanged between those who love one another. It is an expression of fraternal or filial affection. That is why the kiss of Judas in the Garden of Gethsemane remains the supreme irony of biblical history, for with the sign of love and recognition Judas betrayed his Master to the forces of hate and indifference. The symbol of the kiss also came to be important in the life of Francis.

When Francis returned from Rome to Assisi, he had overcome much. No longer did he fear poverty or living on the edge of necessity.

No longer did he desire the embrace of a woman, for he had betrothed himself to Lady Poverty. No longer did he seek glory on the battlefield, preferring instead the banner of the cross of Christ. Yet one fear remained—that of disease, disfigurement, and expulsion from the community—the fate of lepers.

Francis knew from the Scriptures that Jesus had loved the lepers and had touched them. One of the amazing things about Christ was his willingness to associate with those who were the least of society. When John the Baptist inquired from prison as to whether Jesus was in fact the Messiah, one of the proofs cited was that the Lord cleansed lepers. This was appropriate, for leprosy had come to symbolize sin— physical, social, moral, and spiritual decay. Christ had brought renewal to lepers as a foretype of his cleansing of all humankind. Francis, however, still feared to embrace the leper.

Lepers represented the residual fears that continued to haunt Francis, fears that were fed from his remaining pride. A road led from Assisi to a nearby hospital that cared for these rejected and despised persons. One day soon after his return from Rome, Francis was riding on horseback along that way when suddenly he spied a leper. Fear and love struggled with one another in his breast. Francis knew that the moment of moral victory or failure was at hand. Will fought against will. Francis felt a strange power that gave him the strength to dismount and, falling on his knees, to embrace the man and then to kiss the leper's hand.

No longer did the stench of decaying flesh or the sight of a dismembered body deter him from recognizing an immortal soul made in the image of God. Francis did not see a leper on that road—he envisioned the Christ of the Cross. After a moment Francis looked up and was amazed to find that the leper had disappeared. So, it seemed, had his fear. Francis' biographer, Bonaventure, would later contend that the leper was indeed Jesus himself.[10] Francis never said this, yet to the day of his death he would recall the incident as a turning point in his life. Surely by his embracing the afflicted, the Afflicted One of the Cross had embraced him.

The Prayer

Prayer was a crucial experience for biblical personalities. The Scriptures report that Jacob wrestled with God by the Jabbok until dawn. Jesus pleaded with his Father half the night in the garden. John the Divine was "in the Spirit on the Lord's day" and received visions of Christ's purpose for the church. Francis was also a man of prayer. At crucial junctures in his life he, like his Master, "departed into a solitary place" and there prayed. One of these solitary places was, surprisingly enough, a church.

On the road that led from Assisi to the Umbrian plain stood a small chapel dedicated to San Damiano (St. Damian), one revered by the Eastern and Western churches for his charity. Constructed of rough stone in an early Romanesque style and financed by a consortium of noble families, the church had been built near the site where Christianity had first come to Assisi under Bishop Felicianus in the third century.

The place was saturated with history. Mentioned for the first time in a document of 1030, San Damiano is thought to have been erected much earlier. By the time of Francis it was one of many churches across Christendom that had fallen into disuse and disrepair. Bonaventure stated that "it was threatening to collapse with age."[11] The sacred lamp no longer burned before the altar. Daily Mass was no longer said at that table. The walls, now cracked, no longer echoed to psalmody and chant. The roof, having long since fallen in, no longer sheltered a congregation. In the apse traces of blue and gold could still be seen, dimly recalling the church's former glory.

All that remained to remind the worshipper that this had once been a place of prayer were two signs. One was an inscription over the portal as one entered the chapel. The other was a cross that hung over the almost abandoned altar. The inscription read, appropriately enough, DOMVS MEA ("my house"). It represented in a strange way the state of Christendom itself, tottering with age, yet ready for renewal. The cross was an enigmatic sign of the many-splendored reality of the Church. Though Romanesque in form, indicating its origin in the Church of the West, it was painted in a style reminiscent of an icon, which one would find in the Church of the East. There was an almost ironic quality about this cross that harmonized Western and Eastern spirituality, for the two halves of the Catholic Church had excommunicated each other in 1054. The cross spoke, therefore, not only of a broken Lord, but of a broken Church.

Normally one would not have gone to pray in the church of San Damiano. Seeking solitude and desiring a sanctuary, however, Francis sought out this ruin. Bonaventure describes what then took place:

> There as he knelt in prayer before a painted image of the
> Crucified, he felt greatly comforted in spirit and his eyes were full
> of tears as he gazed at the cross. Then, all of a sudden, he heard a
> voice coming from the cross and telling him three times, "Francis,
> go and repair my house. You see it is falling down." Francis was
> alone in the church and he was terrified at the sound of the voice,
> but the power of its message penetrated his heart. . . .[12]

Francis took the command literally. He rose from his knees and
traveled quickly back to Assisi. There he took some scarlet cloth, the
most expensive to be had, from his father's warehouse, and went on
horseback to the neighboring city of Foligno, where he sold it. He
returned to the chapel of San Damiano, where he found an elderly
priest who still frequented the place on occasion. Francis offered him
the money needed for its restoration. The old man, who seems to have
known the impulsiveness of Francis and the stinginess of his father
Pietro, refused to accept the gift. Francis thereupon threw the coins
into a windowsill, where they remained. Then Francis asked the priest
if he could remain in San Damiano. Permission was granted. Many feel
that it was at this point in his life that Francis became an oblate of the
church, that is, one committed to the full-time service of Christ.

Later sources have said that when Francis first prayed before the
crucifix of San Damiano he spoke these words: "O great and glorious
God, illuminate my heart, give me steadfast faith, firm hope, perfect
charity, and knowledge and understanding so that I may keep thy
commandments." Jesus had promised, "Ask, and it shall be given you"
(Matt. 7:7). For Francis the promise became a reality.

The Trial

Trials have often been a familiar experience in the lives of those
who seek to serve God. Joseph was tried and imprisoned; St. John the
Baptist was tried and beheaded; Jesus was tried and crucified; St. Paul
was repeatedly tried and, though often released, was finally convicted
and decapitated. It is not surprising, therefore, that Francis also
appeared in court, there to face a trial.

As a matter of fact, this young man of Assisi was to be tried
twice—once in the town's court and once in the bishop's court. The
occasion for each trial was the same: the outrage and wrath of his
father. Pietro de Bernardone, having discovered his son's theft of his
valuable scarlet cloth, flew into a rage. This was the last and ultimate

insult that he felt his family name could bear. Francis had failed him at every opportunity. His son had been captured by the army of Perugia and had been freed from prison only upon the payment of a large ransom. Francis had abandoned the army of Walter de Brienne for no apparent reason. He had squandered his father's money with feasts, had roamed aimlessly through the countryside, had become the cause for gossip in the marketplace and had persisted in "eccentric behavior." Now he had stooped to something even lower than embracing lepers and fantasizing about "great ladies." Pietro's son had become a common thief.

When Francis next came to Assisi, no longer protected by the "law of sanctuary" which would have applied to him while he lived at San Damiano, his father had him arrested on sight and brought forcibly home. There Pietro cast his son into the dungeon of the house and kept him in chains. Physical abuse was coupled with mental and emotional torment.

When Pietro left Assisi on a business journey, his wife, Pica, released Francis from his bonds. Upon returning, Pietro became violent and apprehended his son as soon as possible. He took Francis before the town court. There Francis made it clear that the secular authorities no longer had jurisdiction over him because he was a "lay brother" and therefore was under the protection of the church. Fearing conflict with the church, the townsmen referred Francis to the episcopal court of Bishop Guido.

Although it was a cold winter's morning, the townspeople quickly crowded into the church square where the trial was to be held. All expected a spectacle unprecedented in the recent history of Assisi. Bishop Guido appeared before the crowd and with great dignity was seated upon the *cathedra*. Over his shoulders he wore a rich and resplendent blue cope trimmed in gold. Here was the embodiment of the power of the church. Guido was a man of middle years, worldly wise and much experienced. Yet he was profoundly moved when the emaciated youth from San Damiano came before him. He heard the charges brought against Francis by his father. Pietro ended his accusations by referring to the stolen scarlet.

The bishop turned to Francis for his reply. Francis said, "Lord bishop, I will not only return the money that I took from him with all good will, but I will even give him the clothes that he has provided for me." With this, Francis stepped out of view of the crowd, only to return stripped of his garments, which he placed, along with the money, into his father's hands. "Up until today I have called Pietro de Bernardone my father. From now on I only wish to say, 'Our Father who art in heaven . . .' "[13] Hushed, the crowd easily could have recalled the counsel of St. Jerome, "Naked, I shall follow the naked cross."[14]

Moved by both compassion and justice, Bishop Guido arose from his throne, stepped down the stairs to Francis, stripped himself of his cope, and covered Francis with it. This act was rich in symbolic value. It was more than simply offering a garment to one shivering on a snowy day. It was an act of acceptance, for Bishop Guido received Francis as a son of the church. Francis now was to be free to devote himself entirely to the service of Christ. The people, we are told, were moved to tears. Before their eyes was fulfilled the saying of Jesus, "If any man come after me and forsake not his father, and mother, and wife, and children and brethren, and sisters, yes and his own life also, he cannot be my disciple" (Luke 14:26). Francis, however, felt himself now to be a part of an even greater family. God was his Father, all men and women were his brothers and sisters, and Lady Poverty was his espoused.

Transition

"There was a man sent from God, whose name was John." It was not coincidence but providence that caused Francis to bear at his baptism the name of the Baptist, the herald of Christ. Like his namesake, Francis would also experience a wilderness. This was not a desert that one could locate on the map. It was, instead, a Sahara of the soul, a search for living water. Like the Baptist, Francis also encountered Christ and felt himself called to a radical lifestyle and ministry. He too was to be a preacher of repentance to a church grown old and a society that had drifted far from its intended destiny.

> The other things that he had heard, however, he longed with the greatest diligence and the greatest reverence to perform. For he was not a deaf hearer of the Gospel, but committing all that he had heard to praiseworthy memory, he tried diligently to carry it out to the letter.[15]

The public ministry of Francis would stretch from his conversion in 1207 until his death in 1226. It is a crowded career, and accounts vary considerably. Legends and history exist side by side. For that reason one must be selective and critical in the use of materials which are available.

The years of Francis' ministry can be organized into three almost equal periods, each of which can be introduced by a symbol that indicates his primary concern in each phase: (1) From 1206 until 1213, from the conclusion of his conversion until the entry of Clare of Assisi into the Franciscan Order, Francis saw himself primarily as "God's Builder" and sought to renew the church of God; (2) from the admission of Clare into the ranks of the Franciscans in 1213 until the controversial convocation called "the Chapter of Mats" about 1221, Francis saw himself as "God's Fool" and desired to share Christ with the world; (3) from 1221 until 1226, from the Chapter of Mats until the time of his death, Francis found himself regarded by others as "God's Light." He was seen as one whose words and deeds mirrored the Christ and illumined both the church and the world.

It is significant that each of these images is profoundly Christological. As Jesus was the Carpenter who died on the tree; the Fool, who embodied the wisdom of God; the Light, which shone brightest from the garden tomb early in the dawning—so Francis was the architect of church renewal, the "madman" who shared Christ wherever he went, the "little candle" whose light was brightest when it was nearly spent.

God's Builder, 1206–1213

Now that he was firmly established in the lowliness of Christ, Francis remembered the command he had received from the cross to repair the church of San Damiano. He was a true son of obedience and he returned to Assisi in order to obey the divine command, at least by begging the necessary materials. For love of Christ poor and crucified he overcame his embarrassment and begged from those who had known him as a wealthy young man.[16]

There is much symbolism involved in the image of the builder. Jesus was a carpenter; Paul was a tentmaker. Early in Scripture God summoned Moses and Aaron to supervise the erection of a tabernacle. Later God commanded Solomon to construct a temple. The Bible reports that the Lord himself was the architect, giving the plans to the king. The Old Testament contains the story of Ezra and Nehemiah reconstructing the walls, the city, and the temple of Jerusalem.

This biblical imagery of building has inspired subsequent generations of believers. Constantine, the first Christian emperor, ordered the building of an entire city dedicated to Christ. In this metropolis, called Constantinople, Justinian the Great, often called the first Byzantine emperor, erected what was for centuries the largest church in Christendom, Hagia Sophia. Upon its completion Justinian is reported to have said: "Solomon, I have surpassed thee." From the earliest times until the present, chapels and cathedrals, conventicles and oratories have been raised. It is not surprising that some Christians have called God "the Architect," naming men and women of the church "his builders."

Although Francis was to become one of the "great builders" of the church, he did not know after his conversion exactly what this meant. It was not clear to him what building entailed. As Jesus, prior to his ministry, retreated to the desert, so Francis, before beginning his work, entered upon his own "wilderness experience." For Francis the wilderness journey occupied two years. During 1206 and 1207 Francis underwent a variety of experiences. Following the trial in the bishop's court, Francis worked his way northward from Assisi toward Gubbio.

One day, singing in French, Francis was encountered by ruffians along the road who failed to appreciate his song. When they asked him who he thought he was, Francis replied, "I am the herald of the Great King." This was too much for the vagabonds, who immediately proceeded to beat him, abandoning him nearby. Recovering, Francis went to an adjacent monastery, where he did menial chores in exchange for his meals.

Finally arriving at Gubbio, Francis started to nurse the lepers in the local lazaret. Even in this act of mercy, however, Francis did not find a full sense of purpose. He was continually haunted by the memory of two dreams. One dream had urged him to return to Assisi, where he would find fully his reason for living. The other dream had commanded him "to repair my house." Francis decided after two years that only by laboring with his hands could he learn what is meant to be a builder and that the location of his mission was Assisi.

San Damiano and Beyond

Upon his return to Assisi in the summer of 1207 Francis sought out the church of San Damiano. Fulfilling literally the imperative "Go repair my house," Francis set for himself the task of rebuilding the ruined chapel. This work taxed not only his time and energy, but his nonexistent financial resources as well. Once, as the son of the wealthy cloth merchant, Pietro de Bernardone, Francis had access to funds with which to purchase the necessary materials. Now, as Francis, the "little poor one of God," he had to beg for stones and mortar with which to refurbish the sanctuary. Wandering the streets of Assisi, Francis encountered former friends and fellow townsmen, and he who once had been "the king of feasts" was now recognized as "the prince of paupers." From them he begged the items necessary for the repair of San Damiano.

In retrospect the return of Francis to Assisi marks an important turning point in his ministry. Like the wilderness preachers before him, Francis had been tempted to live a life of solitary Christianity. John the Baptist, the desert prophet, could easily have been induced to spend his life alone, enjoying communion with God and avoiding the complications of the community. The same alternative appealed to Pachomius, one of the earliest of the great Egyptian "desert fathers." It would have been labor enough for them to "work out their salvation" in social isolation. Both felt, however, as did Francis, the imperative to "social religion" and the necessity to share their life in the society of others. Francis came back from the wilderness as Jesus did, strengthened, filled with the Spirit, ready to preach and to serve.

"Go repair my house." Francis took that command literally. Soon he had rebuilt the church of San Damiano. Following that, he began to repair another ruined structure, San Pietro. Once that mission was done, he turned his attention to the Porziuncula ("the Little Portion"), a small chapel dedicated to the Virgin Mary. But as surely as these years mark the transition in the life of Francis from solitary piety to solidarity with the community, they also reflect his change from one who labored physically with the church of stones and mortar to the one who ministered spiritually to the church of "living stone," the men and women of God. As Jesus was not sent by God merely to be a carpenter working with wood, but a master craftsman of the soul refashioning men and women, so it occurred to Francis that his mission was to rebuild the entire church, not simply the desolate chapels of northern Italy.

This rich insight, with its full sense of mission, came while Francis was at prayer. On February 24, in 1208 or 1209, Francis was attending the morning service at the chapel of St. Mary of the Angels near Assisi. It was the Feast of St. Matthias. The appointed Gospel for the day included these words:

> And as ye go, preach, saying, The kingdom of heaven is at hand.
> Heal the sick, cleanse the lepers, raise the dead, cast out devils:
> freely ye have received, freely give. Provide neither gold, nor
> silver, nor brass in your purses. Nor script for your journey,
> neither two coats, neither shoes, nor yet staves: for the workman

is worthy of his meat. And into whatsoever city or town ye shall enter, enquire who in it is worthy; and there abide till ye go hence. And when ye come into an house, salute it. And if the house be worthy, let your peace come upon it: but if it be not worthy, let your peace return to you. (Matt. 10:7-13)

To Francis these words of Jesus took on a sense of urgency. After he heard them, Francis responded by saying, "This is what I want, this is what I ask, and this is what I yearn to do with all my heart." He then set aside the tunic of a hermit and took upon himself the task of a preacher.

"The Little Brothers"

As Francis had been building churches, so God had been building Francis. In the moving words with which Jesus had commissioned the twelve apostles to work within the Jewish community, Francis found a mandate to witness within the church. He felt himself called to be a New Testament personality with an apostolic ministry. God confirmed this sense of purpose through the events that began to fill his life.

For one thing, as Jesus had called twelve apostles, so now Francis found himself followed by twelve devoted helpers. These companions, who would assist him in his mission, began to join him during the year 1209. On April 16 of that year, two friends of long standing— Bernardo de Quintivale and Pietro Cattani—bound themselves to Francis and his way of life. Many regard this day as the "birth" of the Franciscan Order.

On April 23, Brother Giles, who was to become the most famous of these early followers, became part of the informal fellowship surrounding Francis. More soon followed. Not only did these men finally number twelve, as did the apostles, but they also engaged in the primary work of the early disciples, preaching. Within a year they had conducted preaching missions both in the great city of Florence and in the rural countryside surrounding Ancona. Most of the twelve had come from the "better" or "major" families of Assisi. One of them, Angelo, was a knight. Yet they were no longer to be known as "majors," for they called themselves "Friars Minor"—that is, "friars," brothers committed to preaching, and "minor," the lesser people of society. As the early apostles had identified with the masses, so also did these first Franciscans.

Francis saw that in order to rebuild the church, he must continue to preach. In order to preach, he must be faithful to the Gospel. In order to be faithful to the Gospel, Francis felt he must work within a community, not as an isolated personality. With twelve Friars Minor now attached to him in the work of evangelization, Francis saw the need for some regulation of their life together and of their work in the church. A "Rule" similar to that of Benedictine Order was necessary. One story reports that in order to determine how God wished his small company to be regulated, Francis decided to go right to the Gospels themselves. Disliking formality and fearing legalism, Francis sought out a parish priest and asked him to invoke the Holy Spirit and then to open the Scriptures at random, seeking divine guidance in the selection of pertinent passages by which to govern the Friars Minor.

The account has it that the first time the lectionary was consulted, it fell to this verse: "If thou wilt be perfect, go and sell what thou hast and give to the poor, and thou shalt have treasure in heaven: and come and follow me." Then, turning to the Gospels a second time, this message was read: "Take nothing for your journey, neither have two coats apiece." For yet more guidance the Bible was opened another time, with the result that they found the exhortation of Christ: "If any man will come after me, let him deny himself. . . . " After Francis had listened to these readings, he turned to those with him and said, "Brothers, this is our life and our Rule, and that of all who are going to want to enter our company. Let us fulfill all that we have heard."[17]

Organization of the order from within, however, was not enough. Recognition from without was essential. This acknowledgment by the church could come in many ways. Popular response was evident from the beginning. As with Jesus, so with Francis: "the common people heard him gladly" (Mark 12:37). The clergy and the bishop of Assisi were both favorably disposed toward the Franciscans and did everything within their power to facilitate their ministry.

Nevertheless, this was an era renowned for new movements, some heretical and some orthodox. As these first Franciscans grew in popularity, they attracted attention from beyond Assisi. Many in Italy began to wonder if they were a new heretical sect, such as the Cathari, or whether they were but yet another expression of lay piety, such as that of the Waldensians, which ought to be kept within the bounds of Catholicism. Only one person in Europe in 1210 could validate the Friars Minor as being orthodox. This was the bishop of Rome, the pope or patriarch of the Western Church, Innocent III. To him the brothers would have to go if they wished to expand their ministry and have it blessed by the church.

Although the brothers knew well that they needed the authorization of the pope before they could continue their ministry, many of them were hesitant to appear before Innocent III. His reputation was not that of a particularly progressive pontiff. A cautious man, by 1215 he would forbid the formation of new orders within the church, although some new "societies" of laymen were allowed. The proliferation of orders, sects, and companies had caused much concern in Rome. Furthermore, Innocent was the most powerful man in Europe. No king or emperor could command the respect and the response that he evoked. As he occupied the "Chair of St. Peter" at a period many regard as the apex of the papacy, kings and princes quaked before his power. It was before this man that Francis would have to present his case for the continuation and the legitimization of his order.

While the other friars might well have been fearful, Francis was bold. He set his face toward Rome, leading his "band of penitents" from Umbria to the Tiber. Although the Rome of 1210 was certainly not as impressive as the Rome of today, it was the "See of Peter" nevertheless, the temporal and spiritual capital of the supreme ruler, teacher, and pastor of Christendom.

Upon his arrival in "the Eternal City," Francis had the good fortune to encounter Bishop Guido from Assisi. It was he who made the arrangements for a papal audience in the church of St. John Lateran, the seat of the medieval papacy, and so there, on a spring day, Francis and his friends came to plead their case. Garbed in paupers' robes, barefoot, eyes filled with intense piety, these Friars Minor were a marked contrast to the pontiff and the curial staff arrayed in rich gowns. Making their way down the long, arcaded basilica, Francis and his followers presented their petition to the pope. They asked only to be allowed to live in "an evangelical fashion" according to the Gospels. To everyone's surprise, the pope gave his verbal assent the very next day. He authorized the order.

Since then, historians have debated what Innocent's motivation may have been. Some scholars suggest that the pope's favorable response was prompted by the intercession of a cardinal who was close to the bishop of Assisi. Others point to the pontiff's recognition that in the rising towns of Europe there was a new spiritual force at work among the laity. This energy had sometimes been misdirected; Innocent wanted it to be channeled into the structure of the church.

Still others recall that the pope was deeply impressed by the apostolic piety of Francis and his followers.

This last view is supported by the story of yet another dream in the Franciscan saga. The night after Francis arrived in the audience hall, Innocent is said to have dreamt. In this nighttime vision the pope saw the Lateran basilica tottering on its foundations. Ruination seemed imminent for the temple of God. Suddenly "a poor man, slight of build," rushed forward and propped up the church with his shoulder. This dream profoundly affected Innocent. Many suggest that when on the next day Francis was sent for and came into his presence, Innocent immediately recognized him as the "poor man, slight of build," who had rushed forward and propped up the church. Francis was perceived as a builder sent in answer to prayer, one preceded by an anticipatory vision, one welcomed into the church by popular acclamation. Innocent felt that he had no alternative but to receive Francis as one sent to him from God and to give Francis the official recognition he sought.[18]

With the validation of the papacy, Francis and his friends were now free to work everywhere in Christendom. It occurred to them, however, that up to this point only men had been attracted to the movement. Some noblewomen had expressed interest in this "good cause," but no provision had been made for their inclusion in the order. It was soon to become essential that a place be found for sisters as well as brothers. As had so often happened in the past, so now the next step in the building of the order came about not primarily because of human intentionality so much as because of historical opportunity.

Clare

In Assisi there was a wealthy and powerful family, adroit in business dealings. The name of this house has come down to us as the Offreduccio. As the generations had passed, the members of this clan bore varying names, including Scifi. This is the surname many early biographers attribute to the youngest daughter of Favorone, the head of this portion of the family in the time of Francis.

This daughter, Clare (or Chiara), had been given a name which meant "light." The name would describe her compelling beauty as a young woman. Clare grew to be graceful and slender, with long blond hair falling in curls about her shoulders. Francis and Clare had attended the same church in Assisi, San Rufino, and had been baptized in the same font, which can still be seen today. Her father, like Pietro de Bernardone, was a merchant. It may have been from him that Francis had intended to buy stones with the money he obtained by selling his father's precious cloth. Clare, like Francis, had been destined to marry into the lesser nobility.

Over the years Clare came to know much of Francis and his work. She had been twelve in 1206 when Francis had renounced all his worldly goods in the presence of the bishop of Assisi. Her real attraction to his way of life, however, seems to have come during the Lenten season of 1211. During that time she had heard Francis preach in the church of San Rufino. She was greatly moved by his demeanor, his simplicity, and the sincerity of his address. With two friends she went to the Porziuncula in order to see the restored chapel where Francis and the brothers had taken up residence. There she asked Francis for his advice as to how she could live according to the Gospel. Francis sought to awaken within her the same stirrings that he had felt earlier. For some months they met often and talked about the kingdom of God. A decision would have to be made soon. Clare was now of age to marry, and her family wanted to make arrangements.

One moonlit evening Clare slipped out of her parents' house with a friend. She ran down the streets of Assisi to the little church of St. Mary of the Angels. Francis and the brothers stood before the church with lighted torches and awaited her arrival. Singing psalms, they accompanied Clare into the basilica, where she fell to her knees before the altar and consecrated herself to the service of Christ, promising to live in poverty as Francis and the brothers did.

Clare's golden hair was shorn and fell to the chapel floor. She removed her jewels and exchanged her satin garments for a gray tunic, bound with a cord. Her silken slippers were set aside for wooden clogs. Finally, she covered her head with a black veil. The brothers accompanied her to a Benedictine convent. There she would live until the time that San Damiano could be prepared for her and the other "ladies of the order" who would follow.

These events caused considerable commotion in the community, but Clare prevailed in her determination to lead a life of service in spite of strong objections from friends and family. Later her sister Agnes would join the order. One day even Clare's mother would join the order. As more women were added, they became the forerunners of societies that would gain fame for devotion and service.

Francis called Clare the "most Christlike" person he ever knew.

She would become his most trusted companion and counselor. After the death of Francis, Clare would advise popes, kings, and queens. She was, indeed, to be a "light" that would shine in the temple of God when Francis had begun to rebuild.

Within a period of slightly more than five years, Francis had progressed from being the lone builder of a single chapel outside Assisi to becoming a recognized renewer of the church throughout Italy. A builder is a reconciler and perfecter of varied materials. He fits together wood and stone, lime and clay, taking disparate items and forming them into an overarching unity. Francis as a builder brought together nobles and peasants, knights and townsmen, men and women, to form a movement for church renewal that would spread throughout Christendom and incorporate some 30,000 persons by the end of the thirteenth century. People of varying perspectives, divergent nationalities, different educations, and of many vocations were drawn to the man and his movement, catching his vision of a church renewed and restored, reborn and revitalized. Enormous energies would be released and multitudes would be mobilized by the call Francis felt he had received from Christ to "go rebuild my church."

God's Fool, 1213–1221

My brothers, my brothers, God called me to walk in the way of
humility and showed me the way of simplicity. I do not want to
hear any mention of the rule of St. Augustine, of St. Bernard, or
of St. Benedict. The Lord has told me that he wanted to make a
new fool of me in the world, and God does not want to lead us by
any other knowledge than that . . . I put my trust in him.[19]

Many images have been applied to Christians—they are salt and
leaven, branches and seed, living stones and a holy priesthood. To
Francis, the symbolism of the builder had been especially significant,
for he had felt himself called, like Ezra and Nehemiah of old, to rebuild
the temple of God. As he entered into the fullness of his ministry,
however, another image came to dominate his thinking, that of "the
fool."

Normally the Bible condemns folly. Foolishness is regarded as a
synonym for sin. The psalmist reports that "the fool has said in his
heart, 'There is no God'" (Ps. 14:1). Jesus said of a rich man who had
spent his life only in the pursuit of things and was not rich toward
God: "You fool, this night your soul shall be required of you" (Luke
12:20).

Scripture also recognizes, however, that we live following "the
fall of humanity." For that reason things often appear to be the

51

opposite of what they are. The apostle Paul could write that "the natural man receives not the things of the spirit of God: for they are foolishness to him" (1 Cor. 2:14); he reported that "we are fools for Christ's sake" (1 Cor. 4:10). Folly, from a biblical point of view, can be a virtue under certain conditions. Reinhold Niebuhr, the Protestant theologian, observed, the point is to be able to know the difference between being "a damned fool and a fool for Christ."

Francis was often regarded in his lifetime as a fool by both his friends and his enemies. Those who opposed him sometimes said that he was insane. This is reminiscent of those who accused Christ of mental instability or demonic possession. Those who followed Francis said that he was a "fool for God." Like Paul, Francis was more fond of the foolishness of God than the wisdom of the world.

There can be no doubt that Francis was a nonconformist in many ways. Stories abound that describe his unconventional behavior. Often when Francis felt joyful, he would hold a stick to his chin as though it were a fiddle and dance through the woods and sing the praises of God. On occasions when he was despairing, Francis would have a brother lead him through a town square at the end of a rope, proclaiming that he was nothing more than God's donkey, led by bit and bridle. On still another occasion when Francis was filled with great faith, as before the sultan of Egypt, he would offer to walk through fire to prove the claims of Christ. Yet another time when he was moved with great elation, Francis literally "jumped for joy" before the pope and his counselors. Such conduct confirmed in the minds of many that Francis was indeed "God's Fool."

The folly of God's saints, however, makes us feel strangely uncomfortable. On the one hand, who does not admire a Paul of Tarsus or a Francis of Assisi? Yet our admiration often seeks to limit them to the role of icons. Paul is to be admired in stained glass within a church. Francis is to be entombed in a statue placed within a garden. The stained-glass apostle and the sculpted saint remind us of what we are not, but they do so in a fashion that is not disturbing. It is aesthetically appealing to admire Paul imprisoned in prisms of light, and it is quaint to behold Francis standing in stone among the birds. These experiences are tranquilizing and relaxing and somehow even tend to validate our many compromises of faith.

On the other hand, we would not normally want Paul to be our pastor or Francis to live within our parish. Both men are profoundly disturbing.

What pulpit committee would consider Paul for their congregation on the basis of his record? Here was a man with a history of violence, who incited riots, was often imprisoned, and had neither family nor home; whose faith caused considerable controversy within the churches.

What congregation would normally want Francis to serve on any of its committees? Here was a man of poverty, with nothing to pledge for the annual budget. He owned only one set of clothes, which was ragged and patched. His alienation from his father had caused a scandal in the community. He preached wherever he found opportunity, often in the street instead of the church. He made a snowwoman one winter and called her his wife. He was unpredictable and sometimes would suddenly depart on missions to remote places.

Deep inside we know that should Paul preach from our pulpit, or Francis serve in our congregation, there could be no more "business as usual." We would be called to radical commitments which would not simply inconvenience our lives but would alter them beyond recognition.

Francis felt called to be God's Fool in the world. This would lead him to witness both without and within the church. Where others had feared to go and speak, Francis would move with a boldness that bordered on folly. Let us consider how Francis was God's Fool *without* the church and then *within* the church.

The Mission to Islam

By 1213 Francis believed himself to be summoned by God to be more than a builder of the Temple. The purpose of the Temple is to gather a congregation that worships. While Francis sought to evangelize "lapsed Christians" and reawaken their faith, it now occurred to him that there were multitudes who did not even have a rudimentary knowledge of the Gospel. A sense of mission to those of other faiths now possessed him.

Francis experienced a desire to be a witness for Christ to the Muslim peoples. It was a particularly peculiar vocation, for this was the time of the Crusades, when warfare raged between Christendom and Islam. Many regarded Muslims as candidates for extermination, not conversion. Francis was of a different persuasion, for he desired the inclusion of Muslims within the Temple of God. His was now the task of building a larger house by his witness, a house that would include

Africans and Asians as well as Europeans. Because of this vocation, many considered Francis a fool.

At first Francis' efforts to reach Muslims did appear foolish. There is reason to believe that in the first half of the year 1212 Francis visited Rome once more to obtain the approval of Innocent III for his new missionary enterprises. By the end of that year, after a brief stay in Tuscany, Francis embarked for the Holy Land. He was, however, thwarted in this first attempt. Going by sea, he found the winds contrary, and his ship was driven onto the shores of the Adriatic. After a short time in what is now Yugoslavia, Francis obtained passage back to Italy.

Not despairing, in the year 1213 Francis traveled to Spain, then largely a Muslim land and regarded by many as a part of Africa (one historian suggests that in the Middle Ages Africa began at the Pyrenees). He attempted to pass over to Morocco to preach before the sultan, Muhammad ibn Nasr. This venture came to naught because of Francis' recurring illness. His sickness caused him to return from Spain to Italy, possibly passing through southern France along the way.

For almost five years Francis had to turn his attention to other matters within the order. His mission to Muslims seemed to be postponed indefinitely. The challenge of Islam, however, would not allow his soul to rest. In the year 1219 Francis once more embarked on a journey to the Muslim world. Going to the port of Ancona, Francis and twelve companions boarded a ship bound for Acre in Syria. It was June, still the season of beginnings, and this time his venture of faith would come to fruition.

Little is known concerning the circumstances or itinerary of this journey. We may speculate that Francis and his friends touched the islands of Candia and Cyprus (at that time a Crusader kingdom). In any case, by midsummer Francis was in Syria, where he assigned various tasks to his companions. Francis, however, with a single friar, Illuminato, traveled through the Crusader states established along the Mediterranean littoral, toward Egypt. There a Crusader army was encamped before the walls of Damietta. From August 1219 until February 1220, Francis and Illuminato stayed in the Crusader camp.

The saint of Assisi was shocked at the conduct of these erstwhile "Soldiers of the Cross." Soon he began to preach repentance among the troops. It is a strange coincidence of history that the army was led by Jean, king of Jerusalem, the brother of Walter de Brienne, whom Francis had once hoped to serve before his dream at Spoleto. Francis once more was at war, but now he served as a "chaplain," not a knight, as a vassal of the Prince of Peace, not a soldier of the king of Jerusalem. Although this was not the ministry Francis had envisioned when he went east, it was a challenge for him to share his message of peace with the Crusaders. This, however, was not the mission to Muslims which he had so desired.

For a man like Francis, what he witnessed in those terrible months must have made him recoil with horror. The cross under which he had hoped to unite all men in love was being used as a standard of war. Atrocities committed by both sides were now commonplace. Jesus, who had embraced the stranger, was now a name evoked by those who sought to destroy the children of Ishmael.

On August 24, 1220, the Crusaders were preparing a final assault on Damietta. Francis perceived that the battle would go against the Christians, and he advised the commander to wait. His warnings were ignored, and the attack went forward on August 29, the day that commemorates the death of John the Baptist in church tradition. The Crusaders were slaughtered below the walls of the city. Returning to their encampment, the soldiers were exhausted and demoralized. The Muslims had in fact almost destroyed the army. Arab traders in the city were already offering gold for the Christian slaves who were expected to be taken in the coming days. Amid such circumstances, Francis felt compelled to preach, making clear to the troops both the law of God, which condemns sin, and the Gospel, which offers comfort and restoration.

The siege, however, had only begun. Reinforcements arrived, and the Christian forces regrouped. Muslim expectations of victory were frustrated, and Christian anticipations of the occupation of Damietta were revived. Circumstances changed, and now the Muslims were in deep distress. Food shortages, inadequate sanitation, epidemic disease, and intense despair swept the Arab city.

On November 12, 1219, the Crusaders attacked the town and put it to the sword. Francis was nauseated at the sights he now witnessed. Men were massacred, women were raped, children were sold into slavery. All this was done in the name of Jesus. Francis wondered who was the fool—he, who preached the Prince of Peace, or they, who wrought death in the name of the Author of Life.

Following the fall of the city, the Muslim army under Malik el-Kamil retired some sixty miles to the south. The route for the Crusaders to Cairo remained blocked. New troops began to gather beneath the sultan's banner. The sultan issued a command offering a piece of gold for every Christian head brought to him. It is easy to imagine the surprise of the Crusader commander when, under these circumstances, Francis asked his permission to cross the enemy lines in order that he might preach to the great sultan. After much discussion, permission was granted.

As in the days of his conversion, Francis went through the lines singing at the top of his voice. He was seized almost immediately by Muslim soldiers. Francis began to cry out, "Sultan, sultan!" This he did so loudly that they thought he was an emissary of peace. Francis was taken before the sultan. Many stories are told of this dramatic encounter. One of them reports that the sultan asked Francis if he wanted to become a Muslim. Francis replied that he did not, but instead had come from God to show the sultan the way of salvation.

After a long discussion, Francis offered a test of faith. The sultan could choose his greatest mullas, and Francis would walk through a fire with them. Those who survived would be those of the true faith. The sultan replied that it would be difficult for him to find men who would accept such a challenge. Francis then offered to go through the fire alone, to prove the truth of the claims of Christ. Although his offer was declined, the sultan was greatly moved and sent Francis on his way with a safe conduct to visit the holy places of Palestine.

It is assumed that Francis did indeed visit the sites connected with the earthly life of Jesus. We can only imagine the feelings of the saint of Assisi as he stood in the Grotto of Bethlehem or before the Sepulcher in Jerusalem. He did not commit to writing what took place. All is lost in legend. He returned to Italy in the autumn of 1220.

Was the mission of Francis to Muslims an act of folly? Was it foolish to preach before the sultan or to seek to change the hearts of hardened soldiers in the Crusader camp? From a human standpoint, the whole episode seems fruitless, without rational cause or significant consequence. It appears to be a meaningless ministry. From the vantage point of the Sermon on the Mount, however, the behavior of Francis is probably the only rational and significant conduct exhibited in the whole situation. Jesus had said, "Happy are the peacemakers" (Matt. 5:9). To Muslims, who follow the faith of Islam, the religion of "submission to" or "peace with" God, and to Christian Crusaders, who wore as their emblem the cross, the sign of the Prince of Peace, Francis came as the one who, though a fool for Christ, embodied the wisdom of God. For Francis brought the love of Jesus and sought peace between estranged humans.

The Mission to His Own

While Francis had been witnessing in the world, ministering as God's Fool on foreign shores, changes had occurred at home within the order he had founded. This became tragically evident to Francis upon his return to Europe. In September 1220, Francis and Illuminato made their way to Italy from the Middle East. They stopped briefly at Verona, then went southward to Bologna. Francis was in a state of exhaustion. He was now also plagued with a disease of the eyes, contracted in Egypt. For the rest of his life he would be unable to cease weeping. Ironically this must have reflected his innermost feelings when he saw what had transpired during his absence.

Many brothers had sought to introduce changes in the order. They felt that the Franciscan program of radical austerity was incompatible with an effective ministry to a sophisticated society. Bologna, for example, was not only a wealthy city, but also a place of great learning, celebrated throughout Europe for its university. More than 10,000 scholars of many nations flocked to the school, many of them intending to study Roman Law. Careers beckoned to them in the rising chancelleries of Europe. Francis in 1211 had sent Brother Bernardo here to preach. Bernardo was thought of as a "curiosity"and unworthy of serious consideration. His mission had at first evoked laughter instead of repentance. Although a mission continued in that city, it took on a life of its own.

When Francis arrived in Bologna in 1220, therefore, he found doctors of the university who were Friars Minor, but who continued to hold their academic positions, their homes, and to live a life in the world. They were attracted to the Franciscan movement, but they felt that its methodology was questionable. While they appreciated his noble intentions and the compelling power of his vision of rebirth, they felt Francis had crippled the order by committing it to an archaic lifestyle.

Francis, leaving Bologna, went on to Florence and then to Orvieto, where the new pope, Honorius III, and his court were in residence. There Francis preached before the pontiff and the cardinals. Among the cardinals was one named Ugolino (the future Gregory IX), whom the pope had named as a guide and protector to the

Franciscans. Cardinal Ugolino struggled to show Francis the proper
balance between the divine imperative and human reality. His line of
argument was that the radicalism needed to found the order would be
destructive of the evangelical thrust needed to ensure the success of its
work and of the catholicism required for the order to find a permanent
home within a broad and diverse church.

The dilemma facing these men was as old as the New Testament.
There we find concurrently the radicalism of John the Baptist, the
evangelicalism of Luke the Physician, and the catholicism of James the
Just, elder of Jerusalem. Jesus had called some to austerity, like the rich
young ruler. Others Christ had sent back to the community, like the
Gadarene who returned to his family to bear testimony to his healing.
Still others Christ placed in positions of authority and responsibility,
like Peter and Paul, who were to be rulers in the church. Ugolino and
Francis were caught up in this web of conflicting loyalties as they
struggled with the confusion of establishing priorities. Was the need of
the hour a return to the radicalism of the early days of the order, or
was it the remodeling of the movement to allow it to minister in new
and different ways?

We can only speculate as to the inner feelings of Francis during
this time. His recurring illness which had first taken hold in the
dungeons of Perugia returned. Physically exhausted from his trip to
the East, Francis became emotionally worn by the conflicts within the
order. Francis felt rejected, as if he had become a fool, not for Christ,
but through circumstance. Had his initial vision been one of folly or of
wisdom? Was his vision of a radical Christianity one furnished by the
spirit of self-deception or by the Holy Spirit? Confusion reigned. The
result was that the Rule was indeed modified. Although the revision
was not as thoroughgoing as many desired, Francis felt that certain of
the brothers had gone too far in order to meet the world.

On September 29, 1221, a general chapter known to us as the
Chapter of Mats (due to the rush-fabricated huts that were constructed) was called.[20] A "general chapter" was a meeting of all the members
of the order for the purpose of discussing common concerns. The new
Rule was read. Francis, however, seems to have returned to his original
vision of a radical form of evangelical Christianity. He rose to speak.
All fell silent. His heart was filled with the vision of the Crucified, the
one who had no place to lay his head. Memories of the early days of
the order in Assisi and by the Rivo Torto flooded his mind.

What Francis said shocked the brothers. He resigned from the leadership of the order, saying, "From now on I am dead to you." The brothers began crying and weeping, asking him to remain. Francis, however, responded that he would turn the order over to others and let them render an account on the Day of Judgment for the direction it had taken. He ended by saying that God had willed that he be his fool in the world and that he would follow the path God had chosen for him. Francis left to spend much of the rest of his life in solitude. As he had been called alone before the crucifix at San Damiano, so now he would walk alone once again.

There is a paradox about this period in the life of Francis of Assisi. Never before had he been more involved in the world, witnessing to his faith in many countries and testifying before kings. Yet never before was he to be so alone—rejected even by those who bore his name and lived by his counsel. Like Elijah, who after the magnificent triumph on Mount Carmel faced depression in the solitude of the wilderness, so now Francis, having been a mighty mover of the church, found himself an enigma. He was God's Fool in the world—yet the foolishness of God was not always perceived as wisdom. This fool for Christ would now follow in his Master's footsteps, and that path would lead to a cross.

God's Light, 1221–1226

> He was to be a light for those who believe that, by bearing witness of the light, he might prepare a way for the Lord to the hearts of his faithful, a way of light and peace. By the glorious splendor of his life and teaching Francis shone like a day-star amid the clouds, and by the brilliance which radiated from him he guided those who live in darkness, in the shadow of death, to the light . . . bringing good news of peace and salvation to men . . . Like St. John the Baptist, he was appointed by God to prepare a way in the desert . . . and preach repentance by word and example.[21]

One of the most powerful symbols used by Jesus to describe his followers was light. He had said, "You are the light of the world" (Matt. 5:14). Light was the first of God's creations. The initial words of God in the Scripture are "Let there be light" (Gen. 1:3). Christ rose on Sunday, the "day of light." Jesus spoke of himself as "the light of the world" (John 9:5). John the Evangelist said of Christ that "in him was life; and the life was the light of men. And the light shone in the darkness; and the darkness did not comprehend it." (John 1:4-5). When, therefore, Jesus compared his disciples to light, he was paying them the highest compliment possible. He was identifying them with himself.

Toward the end of his life Francis was described by his followers as "a light." By doing this they meant to say that Francis had become transparent to Christ, the true light. Francis had become like Sister Moon, without beauty of itself, yet filled with grace when reflecting the light of Brother Sun. Francis in the last years of his life was a manifestation of the luminescence of the Christ.

To subsequent generations it has seemed paradoxical that the followers of Francis would ascribe this attribute to him during his final years. This paradox rests on two empirically verifiable realities.

Firstly, Francis in his later years was less active in society than in his earlier life. This man of action, who had founded an order, pioneered church renewal, preached from the Alps to the Sahara, witnessed before sultan and scholar, and had ministered to the classes and the masses, now became a man of reflection. Although only in his early forties, Francis virtually retired from society. To those who customarily regard light as a synonym for labor, it is hard to comprehend why Francis in his last years would earn a reputation as a light-bearer. Did not Jesus say, "I must work the works of him that sent me, while it is day; the night comes, when no man can work. As long as I am in the world, I am the light of the world" (John 9:4-5)?

Secondly, Francis in his later years was afflicted with many diseases. Never a robust man, he now suffered from a variety of maladies. Due to his strict life Francis had developed a gastric ulcer and dyspepsia. After his journey to Egypt he had contracted an illness of the eyes, probably a serious form of trachoma. This eventually would cause Francis to go blind, plunging the end of his life into darkness. As his vision became impaired, it was felt necessary by the doctors of his day to lay a red-hot iron across his forehead to cauterize the veins. This treatment was incredibly painful, and it proved unsuccessful. To those accustomed to light being a synonym for life and health, the afflictions of Francis seem incongruous.

Upon further reflection, however, the title "light" is the only one that adequately describes Francis in his final years. Of course he was no longer a man of action, nor a person of unimpaired health. Yet it is precisely the meaning of affliction that often we most resemble Jesus when, like him, we are stricken and silent, suspended on a cross between heaven and earth. It was when Christ was isolated from society, crucified outside the city walls, forsaken by all save his mother and John, that he gave his most eloquent witness to the world. This the church has seen as the redeeming action par excellence. It was in the darkness of a Good Friday afternoon that the light of the world was made fully manifest. In such a fashion, the meaning of the life of Francis as a light-bearer became fully evident to his friends and followers only in the trouble-filled years of his later life, when Francis sought solitude and meditation.

After the Chapter of Mats, Francis was alone as he had never been before. The dissension and differences of opinion within the order had left him drained of his former exuberance. Francis now desired to live the life of a contemplative, far from the worries and conflicts that had plagued him. Peace was what he needed and longed for, and it could only be found in the company of his Lord. These latter years were to be spent in solitude.

Francis, however, felt compelled to complete a final task before he withdrew from the world. Retreating to a small hermitage at Fonte Colombo, Francis composed yet another set of directions for the friars, one which he hoped they would accept. This writing of Francis encouraged his followers to "let poverty be your party." Although preserved as a document, reflecting his spirituality, this was the only Rule not to be approved by a papal decree and it was disregarded in the regimen of life in most communities.

Francis felt that he had left a legacy—born of prayer and struggle—that he deemed the most precious commodity he could give to the human family. But to his puzzlement and bereavement, even his closest friends and followers, while they hailed him as "a light of God," could not appreciate the gifts he offered them. Their rejection of his expression of radical Christianity, and their modification of it to suit the circumstances of their ministry, saddened him. For him it was not simply a rejection of his own toil, but a serious alteration of the Gospel imperative.

By the year 1224, Francis could sense the approach of Sister Death. He had spent the last two years revisiting the places that had meant so much to him as a young man. We know that he would occasionally return to Assisi during these travels. On one of these occasions Francis sought out the chapel of San Damiano. The sisters of Clare now used the church as a residence and place of ministry.

What had once been a neglected and deserted sanctuary had become home for the faithful. It seemed to symbolize the success of the work of Francis. The church, once in ruins, was now beginning to prosper. Yet, when Francis beheld the crucifix before which his career as a renewer of the church had begun, he was not filled with feelings of accomplishment, but instead, of deep questioning. Had he followed his call in the way in which Jesus had desired? A broken body, a troubled heart, and a wearied soul all conspired to accuse him as he knelt before the altar. The discrepancies between what Francis had wanted in his founding of the order and what that movement had become haunted him. Things had happened, of that there could be no doubt.

What disturbed Francis was that the events which had transpired in the past generation were not taking the shape he had imagined. Francis had longed for a church faithful to the Cross, for leaders within the community who, like Christ, would be willing to be crucified for the sake of the world. Francis wondered whether his movement of reform was still conforming itself to the image of the Crucified.

These questions were not to be answered at San Damiano. In the fall of 1224 Francis retired with three companions to Mount Alverna. This isolated hermitage was admirably suited to Francis' need for rest of body and refreshment of spirit. A small parcel of land on the side of the mountain had been provided for Francis by Count Orlando, a friend of the order. By the time Francis reached the small cliff, he was unable to walk and had been placed upon a donkey. Brother Leo, long his companion, had prepared a hut made of branches built beneath a beech tree. Francis asked to be left alone in that spot and only to be brought a little bread and water once a day. Soon after his arrival, while in the deep rapture of prayer, Francis found the answer to his questions.

What occurred on that September day defies rational explanation. It has been examined in many ways—by psychologists, theologians, physicians, historians, and biographers. All leave something wanting. What transpired in the solitude of the mountain takes on a trans-historical character. It was an intensely personal experience, involving Francis and his God. Francis did not speak of the incident to others and, in fact, he tried to hide the results of what had taken place.

It was reported by those who knew Francis that while he was in the attitude of prayer he beheld a vision of a seraph flying in the midst of heaven, reminiscent of the experience of Isaiah. As the angel hovered above the cliff, Francis felt an intense passion, that is, both pain and joy simultaneously. He then fell unconscious. Awakening later, he was astounded to find that in his hands and feet and in his side he was wounded in a fashion similar to Jesus on the cross. Francis refused to comment on the occurrence to his companions. To those nearest him, however, it was regarded as an answer to his prayers, a final validation of his ministry. He who had sought to conform himself in all ways to Christ was now to resemble the Savior even in his physical appearance.

Francis left Alverna strengthened in his soul, although further weakened in his body. During the next year his health steadily deteriorated. The doctors of his day performed a number of painful but pointless operations in an effort to heal him. Only a man strong of will and possessed of an indomitable spirit could have endured such agonies. His companions finally decided to take Francis to Siena, there to pass the winter months. This sojourn provided no relief. Francis' arms and legs began to swell, his stomach refused nourishment, and his body was wracked with fever. He was afflicted with a multitude of maladies beyond the help of the medical knowledge of his day. In this state Francis begged the brothers to take him back to Assisi. Where he had begun his pilgrimage, there he would finish it.

In May 1226 a stretcher bore Francis from Siena to Assisi. It was already late spring in north-central Italy. Brother Sun was shining in full splendor, though Francis was now unable to behold his glory fully through his blinded eyes. Mother Earth was radiant in all the floral attire of the springtide, yet Francis was now unable to accept her invitation to walk through the fields singing a song of the season.

Francis, in these last days, wrote his *Testament* and reminisced with the brothers, recalling in rapid succession the many events of his life—Lady Poverty, the lepers, San Damiano, the early friars, Sister Clare, and more. As Francis felt Sister Death at his shoulder, he asked to be taken to the Porziuncula, the "Little Portion," the first home of the Friars Minor. There he would end his days. Laid on the cold earth, in the midst of his closest brothers, Francis sang with them the Evening Office of October 3, 1226. At the end of the appointed psalmody Francis in a frail voice intoned the versicle, "Bring my soul out of prison, that I may praise your name" (Ps. 142:7). All was silence. Francis had died.

"The spirit of man is the candle of the Lord" (Prov. 20:27). No one apart from Jesus better embodied the biblical symbol of light than Francis of Assisi. Wherever he went, the qualities of light were evident—warmth and love, wisdom and truth, passion and fire. Those who knew him could say as did those who walked with Christ, "did not our hearts burn within us." His light had illumined the dark places of medieval Christendom—the Crusades, the leprosaria, the dungeons, and the hovels of the poor. To those who "sat in darkness," Francis, like Jesus, brought light.

As a "candle of the Lord," Francis spent himself with great extravagance for the sake of those who needed him. Yet, as Francis was "God's Candle," we cannot say that he will ever be extinguished, or that he can truly die. Another man named John, called the Seer, had a vision on the Lord's Day. He reported that in our Father's house candles still burn bright. Sometimes in the cold and dark of our world, we catch a glimpse of their light, and we take courage for the living of these days.

Two

Meaning

Worship

When you are preaching, too, tell the people about the glory that is due to him, so that at every hour and when the bells are rung, praise and thanks may be offered to almighty God by everyone all over the world.[1]

Francis of Assisi is usually honored more as a renewer of the church than as a formulator of liturgical principles. He has been praised as a reformer of the faith, a champion of the poor, a pioneer of social compassion, an advocate of the religious life, a pathfinder of world missions in general, and Muslim-Christian contacts in particular. Certainly Francis fulfilled many roles—teacher and preacher, evangelist and missionary—but central to them all was his understanding of Christian worship.

There are ample clues to suggest the centrality of worship for Francis, indicating that liturgical life provided the basis for his character and career. He came to a renewed sense of the presence of Christ while at prayer before a Byzantine-inspired iconographic crucifix that was hanging over the deserted altar of a ruined church. His first task was to rebuild that very church of San Damiano. His second project was the rebuilding of a small ruined chapel dedicated to St. Mary (the Porziuncula). It was in this church that Francis attended services on the Feast of St. Matthias, February 24, 1208. The Gospel for that day provided a vocation, not only for Francis, but for all who would follow his Rule of 1221:

> And as you go, preach, saying, The kingdom of heaven is at hand. Heal the sick, cleanse the lepers, raise the dead, cast out devils: freely you have received, freely give. Provide neither gold, nor silver, nor brass in your purses, nor scrip for your journey, neither two coats, neither shoes, nor yet staves: for the workman is worthy of his meat (Matt. 10:7–10).

Apart from Francis' own familiar prayers, he also authored a liturgy of the Hours, *The Office of the Passion*. Some scholars assert that the doxology in the last Rule (1223) of Francis is really a eucharistic prayer. He is the author of widely sung hymns, known and loved in the entire Christian family from Southern Baptists to Anglo-Catholics. Francis introduced or popularized many customs now cherished in the church, such as the Christmas crèche. It is interesting to note that some of the earliest representations of Francis show him vested in a deacon's dalmatic and assisting at the altar. All these writings and incidents are evidence of a liturgical theology that was at the very foundation of the life of Francis and provided a portion of the power of the early Franciscan movement.

Undergirding the life and labor of Francis are four liturgical principles which, we believe, anticipated the work of later reformers like Martin Luther (who himself was taught by Franciscans while at Eisenach in his formative adolescent years) and reform movements like Vatican II. These principles contribute significantly to the renewal of liturgical worship in the late twentieth century: *the sacramental life, the people of God, proclaiming the Word, and service in the world.*

The Sacramental Life

> We clerics cannot overlook the sinful neglect and ignorance some people are guilty of with regard to the holy Body and Blood of our Lord Jesus Christ.[2]

For Francis the starting point of any Christian vocation was the recognition of the centrality of the sacramental life. For Francis, life in Christ's church begins and ends in bread and wine; the Eucharist is the very core; all is centered at the altar. Francis wrote, "Indeed, in this world there is nothing of the Most High himself that we can possess and contemplate with our eyes, except his Body and Blood."[3]

An old English proverb reports, "Bread is the staff of life." Christians need energy—spiritual vitality. Christ said, "I am the bread of life" (John 6:35). He taught us to pray, "Give us this day our daily bread." Paul wrote, "The Lord Jesus, the same night in which he was betrayed, took bread . . . " (1 Cor. 11:23). God provides us not only with Scripture, but also with the Supper. The Eucharist is for our nourishment. A preparatory rite for Holy Communion reads, "The Holy Supper . . . has been instituted for the . . . strengthening of those who . . . hunger and thirst after righteousness."[4]

One exemplary person in twentieth-century Italy thirsted after that righteousness. Ignazio Silone was a leader of the resistance against Benito Mussolini. He was an accomplished author whose writings reflect his pilgrimage from Marxism to Christianity. One of his most moving novels is *Bread and Wine*. In it we read this conversation:

> "I knew your father as a young man," he (the old one) said to Spina. ". . . Sit here, between his mother and his betrothed; and eat and drink, for this is his bread and this is his wine."
>
> "The bread is made of many grains of corn," said Spina. "Therefore it stands for unity. Wine is made of many clusters of grapes, and therefore it stands for unity, too. Unity of similar, equal, and useful things. Hence also it stands for truth and brotherhood, things that go well together."
>
> On Spina's right was his dear friend's mother, a country woman; on the left his betrothed, a worker. He himself, Spina, was town and country.
>
> "It takes nine months to make bread," old Murica said.
>
> "Nine months?" the mother asked.
>
> "The grain is sown in November, reaped and threshed in July." He counted the months. "November, December, January, February, March, April, May, June, July—just nine months. Also it takes nine months for grapes to ripen, from March to November." He counted the months. "March, April, May, June, July, August, September, October, November—just nine months."
>
> "Nine months?" the mother repeated. It had never occurred to her before. It takes the same time to make a person. He had been born in April. She counted the months backward: April, March, February, January, December, November, October, September, August.
>
> She remembered the moment of love in which he was conceived.[5]

Nine months to make the bread. Nine months to make the wine. Nine months to make the person. That is more than coincidence. It is an indication that humanity is made for the Eucharist, the Eucharist for humanity.

Christianity is to be a family, a *koinōnia,* a fellowship. This is suggested in the Upper Room, where Jesus referred to his followers not as "students" or "clients," but as "friends." He then shared himself with them in the mystery of the Eucharist. All church history is an extension of that event, for Jesus himself said, "I will not drink henceforth of the fruit of the vine, until that day when I drink it new with you in my Father's kingdom" (Matt. 26:29). Eschatology, a breaking-in of the consummation itself, is thus connected with eucharistic theology. The church Christ founded is a fellowship of that communion, by which he is present in the midst of his friends until his glory at the *eschaton* is manifested to all humankind.

Carlo Carretto, author of the book *I, Francis,* is a Little Brother of Charles de Foucauld. Once active in secular life, he is now a contemplative. From his life of meditation has come a wealth of spiritual literature. One of his books is entitled *The God Who Comes.* In it Carretto makes the observation that the Christian is much more than *Homo sapiens;* in fact, the Christian is *Homo eucharistica.* The Christian person lives not by reason, but by the Eucharist. Carretto refers to the story of Elijah. "Leave me, Lord," was Elijah's request:

> But, instead, the Lord says: "Get up and eat, else the journey will be too long for you" (1 Kings 19:7).
> This food given to Elijah on the edge of the desert may be seen as the symbol of a food which is to nourish man: the Blessed Sacrament.[6]

On our wilderness journey, the manna by which we are sustained is the Eucharist.

But what is the substance of the Eucharist? Jesus said, "I am the living bread which came down from heaven: if any man eat of this bread, he shall live forever: and the bread that I will give is my flesh, which I will give for the life of the world" (John 6:51).

One August afternoon a traveler stopped in a small English parish church. Admiring its appointments, he was surprised at the shape of the lectern. It was carved to resemble an eagle that he had seen in American churches. The bird, however, was not soaring—as a sign of John's Gospel, it was tearing its side. The traveler read in his guidebook of "the pelican in its piety" and was puzzled.

When the sexton came, the traveler asked him, "What is the

meaning of the carving?" The sexton replied, "Have you not read the book of Job?" Going to the lectern, the sexton opened the Bible and read, "The eagle dwelleth and abideth on the rock . . . [and] her young ones also suck up blood" (Job 39:28, 30). The sexton then explained, "The eagle is a type of Christ. As in legend she fed her young with blood drawn from her side, so we live by the Eucharist, our communion with Christ's death."

Christ is our food—food that we eat, "else the journey will be too long."

Francis recognized and restored the centrality of the Eucharist, saving worship from two imbalances that have existed in both Catholic and Protestant Christianity. The first imbalance is the elevation of the pulpit at the expense of the altar, so that instead of being "friends," Christians are reduced to being "students" and the church becomes a school with a professor-student relationship rather than a family. This was an abuse common to some of the friars and preaching orders in the medieval church and of an extreme Protestantism in the modern church, epitomized by the sanctuary with no altar, only a central pulpit. The second imbalance is the separation of the altar from the people so that they become "spectators," viewing the eucharistic liturgy rather than participating in Communion. This is a danger found in some medieval forms of Catholic Christianity and is evident in certain segments of Protestantism today.

Francis, then, was a renewer of liturgical principles in the church because he restored the centrality of the sacramental life.

The People of God

> We adore you, Lord Jesus Christ, here and in all your churches in the whole world, and we bless you, because by your holy cross you have redeemed the world.[7]

For Francis the logical corollary of any Christian vocation was the participation of all the faithful in worship. Francis wrote, "It is the Father's will that we should *all* be saved by His Son and that we should receive him with a pure heart . . . and that we should visit churches often."[8] This was his application of the Petrine principle of the "universal priesthood" or the Pauline concept of the apostolicity of the faithful. Worship is literally liturgy, "the work of the people."

The Christian tradition is one of the "book"—the open Bible. It also is one of the "table"—with broken bread. Alongside tome and loaf, there is the basin, filled with water. The people of God need water for refreshment. Jesus said, seated by a well in Samaria, "Whosoever drinks of the water that I shall give, shall never thirst; but the water that I shall give shall be a well of water springing up into everlasting life" (John 4:14). That living water is baptism.

Baptism is many things. It is an *event*—the sacrament or rite of initiation into the church. It signifies incorporation into the Body of Christ. It is the event by which we become the People of God. As such, it occurs "once and for all" and is not repeated. Baptism, however, is also a *process*. As the sign of daily reception of new life in Christ, it is a sacrament of continuation. The reformer, Martin Luther, asked:

> What does such baptizing with water signify? It signifies that the old Adam in us, together with all sin and evil lusts, should be drowned by daily sorrow and repentance and be put to death, and that the new man should come forth daily and rise up cleansed and righteous, to live forever in God's presence.[9]

Luther connects baptism and confession, relating both to the daily forgiveness of sins. Baptism, therefore, is not static—simply a past act. It is dynamic—a present and active reality. Using it, we are restored in right relationships.

Dr. Ted Allenbach, a Christian psychiatrist, spoke to a student convocation on a university campus. During the course of the lecture and discussion, students were allowed to ask him questions. One student asked, "What is the greatest cause of fatigue?"

"What do you think?" inquired Dr. Allenbach.

"Worry," said one upperclassman.

"Conflict," said another student.

"Wrong," replied the doctor. "It is unresolved guilt and unforgiven sin."

Dr. Leslie Weatherhead, long-time minister of the City Temple, London, had opportunity to speak to visiting ministers on a variety of topics. One of the topics touched upon was guilt. "Sin makes us sick," Dr. Weatherhead insisted. "Forgiveness restores us to abundant living." Then he illustrated.

In years past, a woman had invited Dr. Weatherhead to visit her gardener. For decades the man had done fine work, but he had recently become bedfast. No medical explanation sufficed. Physically the man was fit. When Dr. Weatherhead went to see him, the gardener was dressed in pajamas, stolidly in bed, in a room darkened at high noon with the curtains drawn. After some fruitless efforts at conversation, Dr. Weatherhead informed the man that he was going to pray, not asking, but simply recognizing God's pardon for sin as a reality. Suddenly the gardener interrupted the intercessions. Amid a flood of tears he blurted out a confession. "I shall not repeat a word of it," said Dr. Weatherhead. "It was pretty ghastly. The man had done some very sordid things. I heard him out. When I was sure we had put all the hurts into words, I spoke the absolution. I reminded him that he had been christened.

"Then," the pastor continued, "I quoted John six thirty-seven: 'Those that come to me I will in no wise cast out.' I went downstairs. Even while I was yet talking with the woman of the house, the gardener came, dressed in his workclothes, whistling as he walked."

Building upon his baptism, the gardener had been restored to a series of right relationships. He was able once more to participate in the life of the community, to be at peace with the people of God.

For Francis, the participation initiated and enabled by baptism was to be expressed in *word* and in *deed* in the worship of the church. It was in word because Francis emphasized response by the congregation and the use of the vernacular. He was a father of the Italian vernacular, the *dolce stil nuovo*. His poems, prayers, and hymns helped to create modern Italian as the books and sermons of Luther created modern German or as the work of Cranmer in the *Book of Common Prayer* brought beauty to spoken English. In deed Francis stressed the role of the laity. The laity were to serve in the worship of the church. The liturgy was a participatory rite of all the people of God.

Proclaiming the Word

> Moreover, I advise and admonish the friars that in their preaching, their words should be examined and chaste. They should aim only at the advantage and spiritual good of their listeners, telling them briefly about vice and virtue, punishment and glory, because our Lord himself kept his words short on earth.[10]

In Franciscan thought the continuing process of any Christian vocation was the recognition of the urgency of proclaiming the Word. For Francis, the Christian life was begun in baptismal water, nurtured by bread and wine, and manifested in Word and Spirit. Francis said that "no one can be saved except by the blood of the Lord Jesus Christ and by the Holy Words of God."[11] Francis saves us, however, from the confusion that has often surrounded the use made of the Word in the Christian community.

Francis was sophisticated enough to understand the multifaceted function of Scripture within the church. Often today there has been a "Word reductionism" within Christianity, so that Scripture is elevated to a centrality in worship, but is then actually used in a very narrow fashion.

In a way that anticipated the grasp of the Reformers and the Vatican II documents on the function of Scripture, Francis explicated a fivefold use of Scripture within worship, recognizing the different functions of the Word for believers and nonbelievers.

There is the Word of Invitation. This is the function of evangelism; this is the Word directed to the unconverted in the world. As a missionary to Muslims, Francis knew this function. In fact, the Rule for his order pronounced in 1221 was among the first to direct missionary activity, telling his followers "to proclaim the Word of God openly . . . calling on their hearers to believe in God Almighty, Father, Son, and Holy Spirit, the Creator of all, and in the Son, the Redeemer and Savior, that they may be baptized and become Christians."[12] Francis recognized this liturgically as being one function of the Service of the Catechumens, to which all were invited. Francis, however, did not make this the central act of Christian worship, as has become the case in revivalistic and media-oriented Protestantism.

There is the Word of Instruction. Francis said, "I beg Almighty God, Three and One, to bless those who teach, learn, or have by them instruction, keeping it fresh to their memory and putting it into practice."[13] This is the function of education; this is the Word directed to the catechumens, those learning the faith, and to believers seeking to grow in wisdom. This instruction is also expressed liturgically in the Service of the Catechumens (the Service of the Word). Unfortunately, in many cases the lecture has become normative in Christian worship, so that again the church becomes a school.

There is the Word of Admonition. Francis believed, "We should confess all our sins but besides this we must bring forth fruits befitting repentance."[14] This is the function of correction and challenge. It is directed to all, and is the use of Scripture to resolve sin and to direct toward righteousness. It is a penitential function and belongs either in a preparatory confession or in the homily. In extreme cases, however, penitence can become the center of the cultus. Penitence without the joy of resolution and restoration is a mere caricature of authentic Christian worship.

There is the Word of Consolation. This is the function of comfort, or absolution, spoken to the faithful. Francis exhorted, "If one of his brothers falls into sin, he should not be angry with him; on the contrary he should correct him gently, with all patience and humility, and encourage him."[15] This serves as a transition from confession and repentance to reception of the mystery of Christ in Communion. Often in Catholic confession or in Protestant practice this has become a substitute for participation in the Lord's Supper rather than a prelude to it.

Finally, there is the Word of Direction. Francis recognized that Christians were pilgrims needing guidance. The production of pilgrim manuals is an old art. One apex of the industry was in the Middle Ages. Henri Daniel-Rops insisted that "no picture of medieval Christianity is complete without some account of pilgrimages." In that "Age of Faith" we are told that "God's travelers" sought out many shrines, such as Canterbury, Cologne, and Chartres. But the three most popular were Jerusalem, Rome, and Compostella. It is said 500,000 pilgrims annually visited Compostella, coming "from every part of the Western world . . . Germans, Flemings, English, Poles, and Hungarians."[16] These thousands were furnished with pilgrim manuals. These books gave all manner of information. Some of it was practical, describing food, lodging, and medical care; some of it was spiritual, teaching about the life of St. James. All of it was essential for the journey.

The greatest pilgrim manual of all time is the Bible. It pilots pilgrims' progress from the Creation to the Consummation. Reading it we find direction for our lives as individuals and as the church. The Bible is the pilgrim manual that explains to us the landscape of time and space. The Bible gives us a sense of destiny. Because of it, we know where we are going. We have a preview of the end of our journey. Our adventure began in the Garden. We continue in the Wilderness. Our goal, however, is "the holy city, new Jerusalem, coming down from God out of heaven" (Rev. 21:2). The Bible also gives us a sense of certainty. Because of it we know not only where we are going, but how we are getting there. We move forward by faith. As Scripture reports, "By faith Abraham, when he was called to go . . . obeyed: and he went out . . . " (Heb. 11:8). Such is the certainty of faith in the midst of an uncertain journey.

Francis was a renewer of liturgical principles in the church because he rightly understood the use of Scripture in a multifaceted way. He was thus enabled to restore to the medieval church around him the right relationship of Word and Sacrament in worship.

Service in the World

> Everything people leave after them in this world is lost, but for their charity and almsgiving they will receive a reward from God.[17]

For Francis, the consequence of any Christian vocation was service in the world. Life begins with water, is nurtured by bread and wine, expresses itself in Word and Spirit, relates to pastor and people, but manifests itself in movement from altar to earth. Liturgy begins in worship, but the "work of the people" continues in the marketplace. Our common communion is the start of personal and social ethics.

Francis recognized the dynamic dialectic of worship. There is action and reaction, or divine initiative and human response. Worship begins with a procession of the faithful going to the altar. We come from the world into the church.

The liturgy continues with the Gospel procession, bringing the Word into the world, to illumine and to empower by God's initiative. The offertory procession of gifts and of bread and wine are our response to the proclamation. These are our gifts that are offered up and then used in the Lord's Supper, where God gives himself to us. In the recessional we again move from the church into the world. We actualize the drama of salvation from Fall to Consummation, from confession to benediction.

The Franciscan author Murray Bodo wrote a biography of Francis entitled *The Journey and the Dream*. In it, Francis is described as a wayfarer. In a sense, we are all wayfarers on a pilgrimage through life. We are all involved in the journey; we are all reaching out for the dream.

Let us consider what a wayfarer is *not*. A wayfarer is not a settler or homesteader. As Christians we are not called to take up residence in the world. Our life here lacks a sense of permanence. As an old Gospel song proclaims, "I'm just a stranger here . . . heaven is my home." A wayfarer is a transient, a traveler.

Let us examine what kind of traveler a wayfarer is *not*. A wayfarer is not a wanderer, one who roams aimlessly. Our travels have a purpose. A wayfarer is not a tourist, a vacationer, a pleasure seeker.

Our journey is for a different purpose. A wayfarer is not a merchant, with a secular vocation, traveling to make money. Our journey has a holy purpose.

A wayfarer *is* a pilgrim, one with a spiritual vocation, one traveling "for religious reasons." Ours is a moral odyssey through time and space with an eternal purpose. A wayfarer is a pilgrim. That is the biblical name for a believer: "pilgrim." Both St. Peter and the author of Hebrews refer to Christians as "strangers and pilgrims" (1 Peter 2:11; cf. Hebrews 11:13). *Peregrini,* "foreigners," is an ancient Latin word for disciples. "Wayfarer" is a good Anglo-Saxon term for "pilgrim."

A wayfarer is the biblical portrait of a saint. Jesus said, "I am the way" (John 14:6). St. Paul taught "the way of salvation" (Acts 16:17), writing to the Corinthians of "a more excellent way" (1 Cor. 12:31). Before the disciples were named "Christians" at Antioch, the book of Acts refers to them as "those of the way." Dean Willard Sperry of Harvard University suggested: "What is religion? It is a way. What is Christianity? It is a way. Who and what is Christ? He is the way. Who are we? Wayfarers."

William McElwee Miller is a most remarkable twentieth-century pilgrim. His journey began nearly a century ago in the shadow of the western mountains of Virginia. It continued through Princeton Seminary to include almost fifty years of ministry in Iran. Stories about Bill Miller still fill that land. It is said that Dr. Miller once walked the five hundred miles from Mashad to Tehran rather than burden his donkey. He was once asked how he viewed his life in Christ. In reply he told a tale set forty years before.

While traveling along the border of Iran and Afghanistan, Dr. Miller had encountered a Muslim sage. Together the missionary and the mullah rode along the narrow path. In the course of their conversation the Persian asked the Presbyterian, "What is Christianity?" Dr. Miller said, "It is like a journey. For that trip I need four things—bread, for nourishment; water, for refreshment; a book, for direction; and opportunity, for service. These are my pilgrim fare. Jesus provides me with these things. I trust him on my way. That is Christianity."

The saint of Assisi wrote to his friend, Leo, "In this one word, this one piece of advice, I want to sum up all that we said on our journey. . . . In whatever way you think you will best please our Lord God and follow in His footsteps and in poverty, take that way with the Lord God's blessing."[18]

Francis was a renewer of liturgical principles because he knew the dialectical relationship between the church and the world and its meeting in worship. It is the relationship between the "journey and the dream," as Murray Bodo wrote:

> To remain on the road too long
> Dims the Dream
> Until you no longer see it
> And the road replaces the Dream.
>
> The Journey and the Dream
> Are one balanced act of love.[19]

"In Spirit and in Truth"

> All-powerful, all holy, most high and supreme God, sovereign good, all good, you who alone are good, it is to you we must give all praise, all glory, all thanks, all honor, all blessings; to you we must refer all good always. Amen. [20]

When Jesus was in a region of Samaria, he took the time to rest at a local well while the disciples went into a nearby town to obtain supplies. At that place, known by the local inhabitants as "Jacob's Well," Jesus met a woman who had come for water. The discourse that followed has served as an evangelism primer for countless Christians. It is interesting, however, to note that the conversation concluded with a discussion of worship—where, when, and how we ought to present ourselves before God. Jesus set the parameters for proper adoration when he told the woman of Samaria, "But the hour comes and now is, when the true worshipers shall worship the Father in spirit and in truth: for the Father seeks such to worship him. God is a spirit: and they that worship him must worship him in spirit and in truth" (John 4:23–24).

Francis was one who obeyed the injunction of Jesus. Though Francis is often thought of as the archetypal religious rebel and a model of "a free man in Christ," he never allowed worship to be used or manipulated for any ends other then the adoration of the Creator. Liturgy—"the work of the people," the worship of the church—was central to the life of the "Poor One of Assisi." Of his nineteen known and authenticated writings, sixteen of them deal directly with the issues of liturgy, worship, and the Eucharist. Every important event in the life of Francis was connected in some way with the worship of God— whether it was the baptismal font at Assisi, the cross at San Damiano, the readings for the festival of St. Matthias, or the singing of a last versicle response before his death. Francis was a person who throughout his life could not be separated from the worship of God "in spirit and in truth."

> Almighty, eternal, just and merciful God, grant us in our misery that we may do for your sake alone what we know you want us to do, and always want what pleases you; so that, cleansed and enlightened interiorly and fired with the ardour of the Holy Spirit, we may be able to follow in the footsteps of your Son, our Lord Jesus Christ, and so make our way to you, Most High, by your grace alone, you who live and reign in perfect Trinity and simple Unity, and are glorified, God all-powerful, for ever and ever. Amen.[21]

Theology

> You are holy, Lord, the only God,
>   and your deeds are wonderful.
> You are strong.
>   You are great.
>   You are the Most High,
>   You are almighty.
>   You, holy Father, are King of heaven and earth.
> You are Three and One,
>   Lord God, all good.
>   You are Good, all Good, supreme Good,
>   Lord God, living and true.[1]

When one thinks of theology in the Western tradition, certain names come to mind such as Augustine, Aquinas, Calvin, Schleiermacher, and Barth. These men expressed many differences in emphasis and interpretation; but they all shared a common commitment to "theology as system." They were systematic theologians. For them the purpose of Christian theology was to provide a comprehensive and inclusive view of God, humanity, nature, history, and destiny. Such a system was to be intellectually sound, emotionally satisfying, and socially significant.

Augustine wrote of the cities of God and man. Aquinas compiled "all known knowledge" into an impressive *Summa Theologica*. Calvin organized religious revelation for the Reformed faith as Aquinas had done for the Roman. Schleiermacher tried to revision the Christian faith as a founder of classical liberalism; but his successors once again "organized his freedom." Barth, in his attempt to establish a "Neo-Orthodoxy," returned to the classic patterns pioneered by previous generations of Protestant and Catholic theologians.

The result of this tradition has been that theology, for many Christians, has come to be synonymous with a systematic or codified approach to the revelation of God.

It is not surprising, therefore, that while many admire Francis of Assisi as a model of Christlike living, few regard him as a formal interpreter of faith. For them he is not a theologian, because his medium was story and poetry, not philosophy and logic. In fact, all our information about the saint of Assisi has been transmitted to us in stories, poems, and letters. For this reason, while many ascribe to him a place in the history of literature, few acknowledge him to be a theologian worthy of study.

Interestingly enough, however, although few have doubted the value and worth of great dogmaticians, the average Christian in both the East and the West has often drawn the greater portion of spiritual sustenance from a different kind of religious writings. The "theologians" of the laity, and indeed of many of the clergy, have been the poets and the storytellers.

It was Dante Alighieri who explored the Catholic faith for many in his *Divine Comedy*. It was John Milton who interpreted the Reformed faith for many in his epic poems *Paradise Lost* and *Paradise Regained*. It was William Wordsworth who, together with the American bard, Walt Whitman, best exemplified the romantic idealism of nineteenth-century liberalism. While Lutherans may have read the *Confessions* and memorized the *Catechism*, it was probably Luther's hymns and his anecdotal *Table Talks* that often furnished them with spicy spiritual fare.

The great English free churches have rarely produced systematicians, but no one would say that Baptists and Congregationalists are devoid of theology. One need only recall John Bunyan's *Pilgrim's Progress* to recognize that theology can be produced in forms other than system. In our own century, much theology has been done by writers rather than systematicians. One need only think of C. S. Lewis, J. R. R. Tolkien, Evelyn Waugh, Dorothy Sayers, Charles Williams, and Andrew Greeley. It is apparent that there is a long heritage of "theology as literature" in the church. Francis belongs to this tradition.

Theology and Literature

> . . . to everyone in the whole world, Brother Francis, their servant and subject, sends his humble respects, imploring for them true peace from heaven and sincere love in God.
>
> I am the servant of all and so I am bound to wait upon everyone and make known to them the fragrant words of my Lord. Realizing, however, that because of my sickness and ill-health I cannot personally visit each one individually, I decided to send you a letter.[2]

It is not surprising that theology can take the form of literature. Christian theology has its roots in the Old Testament, and even a cursory examination of the Jewish canon indicates that the Hebrews experienced and developed theology as literature. When the ancient Israelites spoke about their experience of God, they did so in the form of sagas, stories, sermons, songs, poems, histories, tales, essays, dreams, visions, riddles, allegories, epics, fantasies, chronicles, jokes, personal letters, civil law, liturgies, testimonies, sayings, proverbs, encyclicals, and philosophical texts. Over a period of several centuries an enormous literature developed. Part of it was oral tradition. Part of it became written canon. For Judaism, theology was literature, not system.

The early Christians continued this literary tradition. During the first century of the church, a vast oral and written literature in Hebrew, Aramaic, and Greek came into existence. A small portion of this survives in the New Testament. In it we find references not only to the recorded sayings of Jesus and the preserved writings of Paul, but to other materials which, unfortunately, have perished (cf. 1 Cor. 5:9; Col. 4:16; Acts 26:24). Within just a few generations the early Christian community produced a New Testament corpus almost comparable in size to the Old Testament, which had taken centuries to produce.

Inheritors of the Jewish literary tradition, the early Christians were also appreciative of classical literature. The apostle Paul did not hesitate to make reference to the Cretan poet Epimenides (Titus 1:12; Acts 17:27–29), to quote an iambic trimeter from Meander (1 Cor. 15:33), or to cite the poetry of Aratus (Acts 17:27–29). In addition,

Paul used frequent excerpts from Jewish literature and pioneered early Christian poetry, liturgies, and hymns (1 Tim. 3:16; 2 Tim. 2:11–13; 1 Cor. 15:42–43). Luke, his companion, patterned both his Gospel and his history (The Acts of the Apostles) after the Greek classics.

The mysterious John wrote a Gospel in the mood of the literature of Hellenistic mysticism. Essays or epistles in the form of fine Latin letters also bear his name, as does that strange allegorical tract, the Revelation, which is written in the style of Hebrew apocalyptic lore. Symbolism derived from both Hellenic and Hebrew sources enriched the appeal of this last letter, which was sent to congregations that were already accustomed to having theology presented to them as literature.

Francis follows in this tradition. He is a theologian precisely because he is a figure in literature. A storyteller, he took up the vernacular and spoke to the men and women in the manor and marketplace about the experiences that filled their lives. He then related all things, common and glorious, to Jesus and his cross. By this, Francis became a theologian par excellence. Clerics and college fellows would read Thomas Aquinas, but the masses came to cherish and inwardly digest the stories of and about Francis. Both philosopher and peasant, prince and pauper came to sing the hymns and say the prayers Francis had taught them. No wonder the theologians of liberation among the poor call Francis "the Preacher of the People"!

We cannot contend, however, that Francis deliberately turned to literature as a method of "doing theology." The choice was not freely made; it was the outgrowth of his personality. This selectivity, while not chosen intentionally or as a strategy, proved to be a very effective mode. To us it appears that literature provides seven functions for theology which are exemplified by Francis and the early Franciscans.

1. There is the ministry of reporting. Literature describes and discloses conditions within a country, a community, a society, or a personality.

Biography was one genre employed by the early Franciscans. Regarded by some as "the highest form of history," biography is a biblical mode of theology. The Scriptures are filled with accounts of personalities such as the lives of Ruth and Esther, Job and Joshua. It was in a particular personality, Jesus Christ, that the early Christian taught that God had fully revealed himself. The Gospels themselves are biographical in character. Because Francis and his followers were so intensely evangelical, the biographical model was quickly adopted by them. Much of the teaching of Francis has an autobiographical flavor. His life is his theology. His biography is his testimony to the revelation of God.

This insight has inspired hundreds of men and women of all faiths to attempt to interpret Francis and his beliefs through instruments of biography. One of the first of these was Thomas of Celano, an early Franciscan brother. His two normative lives of St. Francis are memorable and compelling works of literature that remain primary sources for scholars.

Thomas of Celano, a native of Italy born around 1185, first met Francis after the saint's return from the Holy Land in 1215. Prior to Celano's departure for Germany on ecclesiastical business, he and Francis were in close proximity. That is why Pope Gregory IX commissioned Brother Thomas to compose the first known life of Francis. Little more is known of Thomas himself, for, as a good biographer, he has hidden himself in the person he presents. His style is reminiscent of the four Evangelists, for Thomas makes himself known only in passing. The primary purpose is to present a "God-intoxicated" person. Biography thus becomes theology, that is, "discourse about God" and his dealing with humanity. Thomas of Celano stated at the end of his "Prologue" to *The First Life of St. Francis*, "Thanks be to Almighty God, who shows himself in his saints always worthy of admiration and love."[3]

2. There is the ministry of revealing. Literature can penetrate beyond historical appearances to unveil ultimate reality.

Theology is about "ultimate reality," for it originated in the self-disclosure of God; it is his revelation as it comes to us through the "means" of history and nature, personality and society. The universe and all it contains are seen to be permeated with the praise and glory of God, and therefore theology is often presented in the form of poetry. It then becomes doxology. Having crossed the Red Sea safely, the Hebrews brought forth poetry as praise under the inspired leadership of Miriam. David the king, deliverer of Israel, was also a contributor to the psalter that became the hymnal of his people. Mary the mother of Jesus breaks into song in the famed words of the Magnificat soon after learning that she is to bring forth the Christ.

Francis stands in this tradition. For him theology was often presented as poetry. This is reminiscent of the reformer Martin Luther, who composed hymns; John Donne, divine and poet; and even St.

Thomas Aquinas, who, though known as a "systematician," is also remembered for his sacred verse. The most familiar poem of Francis of Assisi is "The Canticle of Brother Sun." Filled with a sense of holy awe and divine wonder, Francis celebrated all creation. The canticle was a continuing work in Francis' life. He commenced its composition in late life; he completed it almost at the hour of his death. This poem, so reminiscent of the psalter, is the *summa theologica* of the saint of Assisi:

The Canticle of Brother Sun

Most high, all-powerful, all good, Lord!
  All praise is yours, all glory, all honour
  And all blessing.
To you, alone, Most High, do they belong.
  No mortal lips are worthy
  To pronounce your name.
All praise be yours, my Lord, through all that you have
    made,
  And first my Lord Brother Sun,
  Who brings the day; and light you give to us through
    him.
How beautiful is he, how radiant in all his splendor!
  Of you, Most High, he bears the likeness.
All praise be yours, my Lord, through Sister Moon and
    Stars;
  In the heavens you have made them, bright
  And precious fair.
All praise be yours, my Lord, through Brothers Wind and
    Air,
  And fair and stormy, all the weather's moods,
  By which you cherish all that you have made.
All praise be yours, my Lord, through Sister Water,
  So useful, lowly, precious and pure.
All praise be yours, my Lord, through Brother Fire,
  Through whom you brighten up the night.
  How beautiful is he, how gay! Full of power and
    strength.
All praise be yours, my Lord, through Sister Earth, our
    mother,
  Who feeds us in her sovereignty and produces
  Various fruits with coloured flowers and herbs.
All praise be yours, my Lord, through those who grant
    pardon
  For love of you; through those who endure
  Sickness and trial.
Happy are those who endure in peace,

By you, Most High, they will be crowned.
All praise be yours, my Lord, through Sister Death,
    From whose embrace no mortal can escape.
Woe to those who die in their sin.
    Happy those she finds doing your will!
The second death can do no harm to them.
    Praise and bless my Lord, and give him thanks,
And serve him with great humility.[4]

3. There is the ministry of clarifying. Literature can enable the
reader to find moral, mental, or spiritual certainty in a fashion not
always afforded by other forms of communication.

Already in the Old Testament, biblical authors employed
parables and moral stories in order to overcome barriers to understanding. Jesus often taught the people with parables. Who can ever forget
how Jesus shocked the Jewish lawyer by telling him a short story about
an incident on the Jericho Road?

Francis, like Jesus, was also a storyteller. For him the secret of the
Christian life was joy, a "secret" that was difficult to explain to others.
One day Francis walked with Brother Leo along an Italian road. As
they traveled, Francis told Leo a story about perfect joy:

> "Write what true joy is," Francis said. "A messenger comes and
> says that all the masters of theology in Paris have joined the
> Order—write: that is not true joy. Or all the prelates beyond the
> mountains, archbishops and bishops, or the King of France and
> the King of England have joined us—write: that is not true joy.
> Or that my friars have gone to the unbelievers and have converted
> all of them to the faith; or that I have so much grace from God
> that I heal the sick and I perform many miracles. I tell you that
> true joy is not in all of those things."
>
> "But what is true Joy?"
>
> "I am returning from Perugia and I am coming here at night, in
> the dark. It is winter time and wet and muddy and so cold that
> icicles form at the edges of my habit and keep striking my legs,
> and blood flows from the wounds. And I come to the gate, all
> covered with mud and cold and ice, and after I have knocked and
> called for a long time, a friar comes and asks: 'Who are you?' I
> answer: 'Brother Francis.' And he says: 'Go away. This is not a
> decent time to be going about. You can't come in.'
>
> "And when I insist again, he replies: 'Go away. You are a simple
> and uneducated fellow. From now on don't stay with us any
> more. We are so many and so important that we don't need you.'
>
> "But I still stand at the gate and say: 'For the love of God, let
> me come in tonight,' and he answers: 'I won't. Go to the Crosiers'
> place and ask there.'

> "I tell you that if I kept patience and was not upset—that is true
> joy and true virtue and the salvation of the soul."[5]

4. There is the ministry of sharing. Literature is capable not only of communicating ideas and feelings, but also of generating community. When Christians gather as the church, literary forms are employed that bind us to God and to each other. One of the prayers in many services is called "the Collect," for it "gathers together" the sentiments and thoughts of the day. There is the "Prayer of the Church," which touches the lives of the faithful and unites them in common supplication before God. The sermon, preeminently, has the paradoxical role of being both the personal witness of the preacher and at the same time the public proclamation of the people. Preaching therefore becomes more than an individual act; it is a liturgical event, the work of the whole congregation.

Like Jesus, Francis preached wherever he found hearers. An itinerant evangelist, Francis shared in open fields and crowded market squares. A random collection of people would gather. Yet, by the power of his message Francis turned them into a congregation, filled with one holy purpose. They came as the many, motivated by contradictory desires. They left as one, permeated with sacred intentions.

Once, for instance, Francis was preaching to the brothers in the countryside. On that summer day, while the saint spoke, swallows started to sing. The beauty of their song was a distraction from the wisdom of his words. Francis immediately seized upon the opportunity provided him. What could have been disruption became an occasion for instruction. Pausing, Francis turned from the people to preach to the swallows. While he seemed to be addressing the birds, the sermon was in fact intended for humans.

> My brother birds, you should praise your Creator very much and
> always love him; he gave you feathers to clothe you, wings so that
> you can fly, and whatever else was necessary for you. God made
> you noble among his creatures, and he gave you a home in the
> purity of the air; though you neither sow nor reap, he nevertheless
> protects and governs you without any solicitude on your part.[6]

5. There is the ministry of provoking. Literature can challenge. It can call into question unexamined assumptions. It can disclose unworthy motivations. It can inspire moral courage and invite ethical action. It can facilitate reformation.

Nathan, although the court preacher, did not hesitate to confront David with his adultery. John the Baptist, although the son of a priest, did not withhold himself from the severe criticism of the religious establishment. These histories, preserved in sacred Scripture, have informed reformers of every generation. St. Theresa of Avila, although a member of an ancient Spanish family, did not mince words when she described the corruption of her time. St. Catherine of Siena, although a friend of popes, did not cease from telling them of their duties to the church. These are evidences that literature as history can cause divinely inspired discontent and renewed theological reflection.

The history of Francis remains one of the most disturbing of all. There is something profoundly provocative about this apparently meek and mild person. His life calls into question everything that we normally cherish. Even those closest to him were not immune from his "righteous anger."

A most memorable event in Francis' history occurred toward the end of his life. As we have recalled in his biography, by this time Francis had resigned from any role of leadership in the order he had founded. The Rule which he had written in 1221 and revised in 1223 was now being ignored by many of the brothers. Many Franciscans, called from the world, had once again become part of the world. The vision of the founder was no longer being fulfilled. As he lay dying in 1226, Francis produced a last piece of literature, his *Testament*. For those who were close to him, many of comments must have seemed scathing, for Francis recalled his original intentions for the order and placed them before the brothers with stark clarity. The disparity between their deeds and his words became painfully apparent.

> When God gave me some friars, there was no one to tell me what I should do; but the Most High himself made it clear to me that I must live the life of the Gospel. I had this written down briefly and simply. . . . Those who embraced this life gave everything they had to the poor. They were satisfied with one habit which was patched inside and outside, and a cord, and trousers. We refused to have anything more. . . . We made no claim to learning and we were submissive to everyone. I worked with my hands and I am still determined to work. . . .
>
> The friars should not say, this is another Rule. For this is a reminder, admonition, exhortation, and my testament which I, Brother Francis, worthless as I am, leave to you, my brothers, that we may observe in a more catholic way the Rule we have promised to God.

In virtue of obedience, I strictly forbid any of my friars, clerics or lay brothers, to interpret the Rule of these words, saying, "This is what they mean." God inspired me to write the Rule and these words plainly and simply, and live by them, doing good to the last.[7]

6. There is the ministry of healing. Literature can have a therapeutic capacity.

Scripture is read in the church for the mending of the mind and the healing of the heart. The Word, often spoken in dialogue, can bring forgiveness of sin and peace of soul. The New Testament reports "great dialogues," as those of Christ and the woman at the well, or Paul with the Philippian jailer. Who can forget the memorable conversation of Jesus with Nicodemus or that of Philip and the Ethiopian statesman?

Francis was given to dialogue. Through the give and take of conversation the Gospel was communicated. One familiar illustration of this process is provided by the fourteenth-century editor of *Fioretta* ("The Little Flower"), a collection of stories about Francis. Here we learn how God spoke to Francis about the justification of the sinner, in a conversation he had with Brother Leo:

> One night when they got up to recite matins, St. Francis said to Brother Leo: "Dear Brother, we have no breviary with which to say matins, but so as to spend the time in praising God, I will say something and you must answer what I tell you, and be careful not to change words. I will say this, 'Oh Brother Francis, you have done so much evil and sin in the world that you deserve hell'— and you, Brother Leo, shall answer: 'It is true that you deserve the depths of hell.'"
>
> And the very pure-hearted Brother Leo replied with the simplicity of a dove: "All right, Father. Begin in the name of the Lord."
>
> Then St. Francis began to say: "Oh, Brother Francis, you have done so many evil deeds and sins in the world that you deserve hell."
>
> And Brother Leo answered: "God will perform so much good through you that you will go to paradise."
>
> And St. Francis said: "Don't say that, Brother Leo! But when I say, 'Oh, Brother Francis, you have done so many wicked things against God that you deserve to be cursed by God,' then you answer this way: 'You certainly deserve to be placed among the damned.'"
>
> And Brother Leo replied: "I shall do so, Father."

Then St. Francis said aloud, crying and sighing and beating his breast: "Oh, my Lord God of heaven and earth, I have committed so many evil deeds and sins against You that I deserve to be utterly damned by You."

And Brother Leo answered: "Oh, Brother Francis, God will make you such that you will be remarkably blessed among the blessed."

St. Francis wondered why Brother Leo always answered just the opposite of what he had told him to say, and he scolded him, saying: "Why don't you answer as I tell you, Brother Leo? I command you under holy obedience to answer what I tell you. I will say: 'Oh, wicked little Brother Francis, do you think God will have pity on you, for you have committed too many sins against the Father of mercy and the God of all consolation for you to deserve any mercy?' And you Brother Leo, little lamb, answer: 'You certainly are not worthy of finding mercy.' "

And then Brother Leo answered: "Go ahead, Father, because I will say just what you tell me."

And St. Francis, kneeling down and lifting his hands toward the Lord and looking up to heaven with a joyful expression, said very sadly: "Oh, Brother Francis, you great sinner—oh, you wicked Brother Francis, do you think God will have mercy on you, for you have committed so many sins?"

But Brother Leo answered: "God the Father, whose mercy is infinitely greater than your sins, will be very merciful to you and moreover will give you many graces."

At this reply St. Francis was gently angry and patiently troubled, and he said to Brother Leo: "Brother, why have you dared to go against obedience and to have already answered so many times the opposite of what I told you?" And then Brother Leo exclaimed very humbly and reverently: "God knows, dear Father, that each time I have resolved in my heart to answer as you told me, but God makes me speak as pleases Him and not as pleases me."

But Francis was amazed at this and said to him: "Brother, I beg you to answer me this time as I tell you."

Brother Leo replied: "Go ahead, in God's name, for this time I will answer as you wish."

And St. Francis cried out, weeping: "Oh, wicked little Brother Francis, do you think God will have mercy on you?"

Brother Leo answered: "Yes, Father God will have mercy on you. Also, you will receive great grace from God for your salvation, and he will exalt and glorify you for all eternity, because 'whoever humbles himself shall be exalted'—and I cannot say anything else because God is speaking through my mouth!"

And they stayed up until dawn in this humble contest, with many tears and great spiritual consolations.[8]

7. There is the ministry of resolving. Literature can be a medium by which people reflect on the significance of their experiences.

One type of literature employed for this purpose is the journal. Famous religious leaders as different as St. Theresa, Fénelon, John Wesley, and Dietrich Bonhoeffer have kept journals. Through the medium of daily, monthly, and yearly reflection on their experiences, these persons determined God's continuing will for their lives. These journals are reminiscent of those passages in the Pauline epistles where the apostle explores his own experience with others.

Francis as a biblical personality and churchman stood in this tradition. While he employed biography and poetry, story and homily, history and dialogue to teach the faith, the thoughts that could have been included in a journal were yet another mode of theology for him.

> This is how God inspired me, Brother Francis, to embark upon a life of penance. When I was in sin, the sight of lepers nauseated me beyond measure; but then God himself led me into their company, and I had pity on them. When I had once become acquainted with them, what had previously nauseated me became a source of spiritual and physical consolation for me. After that I did not wait long before leaving the world.
>
> And God inspired me with such faith in his churches that I used to pray with all simplicity, saying, "We adore you, Lord Jesus Christ, here and in all your churches in the whole world, and we bless you, because by your holy cross you have redeemed the world."[9]

The Function of Literature as Theology

> It is my desire to relate in an orderly manner, with pious devotion and with truth as my first consideration and guide, the acts and the life of our most blessed father Francis. But in as much as no one can retain fully in his memory all the things that Francis did and taught, I have tried . . . to set forth as well as I can, though indeed with unskilled words, at least those things that I have heard from his own mouth or that I have gathered from faithful and trustworthy witnesses. I wish, however, that I might truly deserve to be a disciple of him who always avoided enigmatic ways of saying things and who knew nothing of the ornaments of language![10]

In the Franciscan tradition, as we have already noted, theology is presented as literature. This literature may be in a variety of modes. We have listed but seven. The next question that arises is this: what is the function of this theological genre of literature? What is the end purpose of a story, poem, parable, essay, or anecdote when related in a theological framework? In the following section we want to examine six results of the use of literature as theology. Each of these relates to the Franciscan heritage; each relates to a revisioning of theological reflection for twentieth-century Christians. The list we present is not all-inclusive, but merely suggestive of ways in which "Franciscans" of all times and traditions may use prose and verse.

1. The Franciscan heritage views theology as an act of invitation. A story is told about Francis going to a town named Gubbio and talking to a wolf who had been terrorizing the community. As a result of the conversation, harmony was restored between the citizens of the town and this denizen of the fields. It is essentially an adventure story, yet it is also an invitation to action. The invitation is for men and women to help restore the primordial balance between humankind and the animal kingdom. Each of us is invited to play a part in this environmental adventure.

This differs from much of Western thought. Many in the Western tradition have advised prescription as the basis of being. The problem is that prescription is usually of the caliber of legislation, a "demand" made on those who are often unable to respond. The "invitation" of the Franciscan tradition is of the same character as the Gospel invitation of Christ himself, for with the summons to action comes the power to transcend the past and actualize the future within the present. The excitement is similar to that of William James's description of the universe as "an unfinished skyscraper." We are called, each of us as skilled in differing crafts, to add our part to the ongoing act of creation.

2. The Franciscan heritage views theology as an act of celebration. While much of Western theology has been serious (there is little humor in either the medieval or Puritan divines), there have been some who thought in terms of a theology of joy. Elton Trueblood, a Quaker, has shown the relationship between meditation, mysticism, prayer, ritual, play, and festivity. In one of his books he boldly explored *The Humor of Christ*. Trueblood has even suggested that some of the parables of Jesus originated as humorous anecdotes.

Many of the stories that have come to us concerning Francis are filled with humor. Francis knew the joy of dancing through the woods, matching wits with the sultan, catching himself in moods of inflated self-importance, and deflating his ego with a gentle hand of humor.

Francis faced affliction and hardship during much of his life and was not ashamed to "go through the world weeping" for the passion of Christ.[11] Yet he was also a man of joy. It is almost impossible to reflect upon the saint of Assisi without a smile. His joy and his humor were unforced. They did not come at the expense of others. Instead they came from an inner childlike quality of spontaneity and an essential optimism. In the stories about Francis we find that it was difficult for him to take the world with ultimate seriousness. Rightfully so, for the world is but a medium for the ultimate, who is God.

3. The Franciscan heritage views theology as an act of introspection. All that Francis wrote, whether Rule, poetry, or letters, arose from personal reflection. It is impossible to read his later descriptions of the spiritual life without remembering the struggles he went through as a young man. When he commands the friars to live in poverty, we recall the scene in the bishop's court. When he advises them to care for lepers, we recall Francis embracing the afflicted one on the road outside Assisi. When he encourages brothers to become missionaries to Islam, we recall his dramatic entry into the tent of the sultan.

Reflection, or introspection, causes individuals to find a universe of meaning within themselves and their experiences with God. Others, outside the Franciscan tradition, have used literature to contemplate this newfound cosmos. Theologians such as St. Theresa of Avila in *The Interior Castle* have illustrated the power of both visionary imagination and autobiographical recollection in a single work. Some, like Washington Gladden, the American Congregationalist, used novels as an extension of his inner self in order to direct society toward alternative models of development. Francis, Theresa, and Gladden are all examples of what the Anglican writer Dorothy Sayers once observed: that it is in creativity that we most approximate the God we name as "the Maker of heaven and earth."

4. The Franciscan heritage views theology as an act of exploration. In exploration we delve into the past to discover causes; we look into the future to anticipate results; we experience the present as the frontier between heritage and destiny. It is interesting to note that in the legends concerning Francis there is much emphasis on prophetic tidings about his birth and ministry as well as a number of prophecies reportedly given by Francis about the future of the order. Francis himself developed certain pieces of literature over long periods of time. As we have mentioned, some of his works like "The Canticle of

Brother Sun" took years to complete and mirrored his life from conversion to death.

While most Western theologies have focused on purpose (as in the issue of predestination in historic Calvinism), some like that of Francis have attempted to cope with the mystery of personal and social destiny. For the saint from Assisi, the "plot line" of God was indeed subtle. He knew this from his own life experiences and from what eventually took place in the order he had founded. God often worked as much through the seemingly "accidental" as the "intentional." This is reflected consistently in the Franciscan corpus. It is reminiscent of the literature of St. Augustine of Hippo who, like Francis, employed story and testament to explain his conversion (*The Confessions*). Augustine also, like Francis, explored the meaning of public as well as personal events. His *City of God* offered in prose and verse a perspective on the reasons for the deterioration of Roman society. Story in both cases lent itself well to the task of theology.

5. The Franciscan heritage views theology as an act of explanation. Theology may be a chronicle that recalls the acts of God and the events that have taken place among his people. When narration of these events is provided, it offers history or tradition. Francis drew heavily on the tradition that came before him and, paradoxically, before his death he had become a tradition in and of himself. By 1226 he was a living institution. Histories would be written about him within a dozen years. Tradition and history may be either the dead letter of the law or the living stream of life. Francis and Franciscan history embody the best of the latter category.

While most Protestant theology has stressed the Scriptures (often at the expense of the collective experience of the Christian community), Oriental, Orthodox, and Roman Catholic teachers have looked more toward tradition. Perhaps in the twentieth century those of the evangelical and Catholic schools can help one another. Today there is often a total repudiation of the past (the annihilation of history), or an irrational restoration of ancient customs without either critical examination or conscious appreciation (the petrification of history). The results are stifling to mind and spirit.

Nicolai Berdyaev, an Eastern Orthodox theologian, lived through the conflagration of the Russian Revolution and struggled with the intransigence of oriental traditionalism. He also puzzled over the Protestant ambivalence toward time (either repudiation in the timeless Idealism of Plato, or adulation in the limitless Progress of

Charles Darwin). By his writing of such books as *The Meaning of History*, Berdyaev, who resided in France, has provided us with an understanding of theology as history, God's extension into time.

Francis was a product of experiences similar to those of Berdyaev. Although he was a Latin living in a Roman Catholic country, Francis was influenced by the Byzantine heritage of faith, was familiar with Islamic customs, and was sympathetic to the rising lay piety of his era. Francis, however, encompassed history in his theology, for history was an ongoing story to which he could write new chapters. History and its record *could* encompass the life of God among humankind.

6. The Franciscan heritage views theology as an act of liberation. Since biblical times the Christian interpreter has faced two temptations. One is to justify the status quo and to identify the extant with the divine; the other is to accuse the system of total inequity and to identify it with the demonic. Both these postures fail to communicate effectively to the majority of people within a society and are normally incapable of producing significant change.

While much Western theology has been an apologia, a defense of the status quo (after all, J. B. Bossuet set forth the doctrine of the divine right of kings with powerful cogency), there have been those, like Francis of Assisi, who with subtle stories and insightful songs have so undermined the established authorities in church and state that liberty became the inevitable consequence. This is surely in the spirit of the Christ, who lived under a foreign despot (the Roman emperor) and a local tyrant (Herod) and who belonged to a religious community that on the one hand manifested rigorous adherence to the law (the Pharisees) and on the other demanded ritual in the temple (the Sadducees). For Christ and for Francis, the function of theology as story was a means of nonviolent emancipation of the oppressed. Theology as literature could lead to liberation.

Reality, Theology, and Literature

> The bishop brought Francis before the lord pope and the reverend cardinals; and standing before such great princes, after receiving their permission and blessing, he began to speak fearlessly. Indeed, he spoke with such great fervor of spirit, that, not being able to contain himself for joy, when he spoke the words with his mouth, he moved his feet as though he were dancing, not indeed lustfully, but as one burning with the fire of divine love, not provoking

laughter, but drawing forth tears of grief. For many of them were
pierced to the heart in admiration of divine grace and of such
great constancy in man.[12]

Measured by the methodology of Thomas Aquinas or of John
Calvin, Francis of Assisi is not a theologian. Theology, however, is
meant to minister to all people. It is to help each person, regardless of
one's educational attainment, to understand the ways of God.
Understanding is not entirely cerebral, nor is it solely intellectual. For
the majority of Christians it is devotional and practical. With this in
mind, who can doubt the theological impact of the hymn "The
Canticle of Brother Sun" or the story of "Perfect Joy"?

The literature about Francis continues to make a theological
impact on the lives of contemporary men and women. Francis has
inspired countless biographers. Even the medium of film has been used
by Franco Zeffirelli to retell the story, in the movie *Brother Sun, Sister
Moon*. Today, as in the biblical age and the medieval era, men and
women respond to theology taught through literature; and in parable
and poetry, narrative and short story they experience the reality of God
in both the extraordinary and the commonplace.

Society

To all Christians, religious, clerics and lay folk, men and women; to everyone in the world, Brother Francis, their servant and subject, sends his humble respects, imploring for them true peace from heaven and sincere love in God.[1]

Life is lived in community. From time immemorial we have spelled out the relationships that confirm and fulfill human personality. Confucius spoke of five dialectical relationships as the foundation of society: (1) husband-wife, (2) parent-child, (3) businessman-client, (4) teacher-student, and (5) king-subject. Philip Melanchthon wrote in the sixteenth century of persons existing in the "natural orders" of the family, the state, and the academy. There is a similarity here to the thought of Francis, who, although recognizing that personal identity extends beyond institutions, yet as a person of love lived in relationships with others. Francis in his very life held the creative tension of what it means to be an individual Christian in a complex society.

It is no accident that Francis is credited with the Christmas crèche. We know that he was devoted to Mary the mother of Jesus, that he was especially fond of the Feast of the Nativity, and that he loved children, sometimes wishing he had some of his own. The order he founded was an "extended" family in which familial terminology was central.

The Family

> Let each member fortify his household to serve God.[2]

One would not be exaggerating to say that for Francis, family was crucial to his vision of the new humanity. Yet this is a paradox, for at least two reasons.

The first is that Francis did not come from a happy home. As a young man Francis was constantly at odds with his father. After his conversion, Francis' parents and any siblings he might have had fade from view and are heard from no more. There seems to have been little in his father that modeled for Francis the loving and gracious God of Christian faith. It is no surprise, therefore, that Francis, standing before the bishop of Assisi, renounced his earthly father's name and possessions in favor of his "Father in Heaven."

The second reason for this paradox is that Francis never founded his own home or family, for he chose a life of celibacy. The yearnings for family, however, seem to have often laid their claim on Francis. On a winter's day when these feelings came upon him, we are told, he constructed a family out of snow. One figure was his "wife" and the others his "children." After fashioning this "family," Francis contemplated how he would have to take care of them all and leave the life of poverty that he had chosen. It is said that at the end of this episode he decided that he much preferred his state of celibacy!

The key to these events is the concept of volitional choice. Francis had chosen the "radical alternative" that was symbolized by Jesus, Paul, the prophetic wilderness preachers (like John the Baptist) before them, and the desert fathers after them. Thus, one should not be misled into thinking that Francis did not value domesticity, or that his ethic has little to say about the role of the family in which people find their birth and growth, their service and death.

Most of us live in families. Francis recognized this when, in 1221, he formed a Rule for a Third Order of Franciscans. The First Order had been created for men who would take vows of celibacy, as later the Second Order would be formed for women with a similar vocation. The Third Order, however, was designed for married couples and families who wished to live the "gospel life" of devotion to

God and humanity in the world, retaining their jobs and obligations. This showed the high regard of Francis for the family unit and its continuation.

No one would have accused Jesus of not having much to say about the family. The philosophy of St. Paul on marriage, although debated, is still important in world Christianity. Francis followed in the steps of Christ and the apostle in formulating a Franciscan ethic of family. This ethic contains two points.

1. The family is an intentional community. Like medieval theologians, Francis recognized that marriage and the family are not accidental—that is, something capricious or an unreasonable act of history. The family is written into the very fabric of nature. It is intentional in that God planned it. In the Genesis account of creation we read:

> And the Lord God said, It is not good that the man should be alone; I will make him an help meet for him. . . . And God created a woman, and brought her to the man. And Adam said, This is now bone of my bones, and flesh of my flesh. . . . Therefore shall a man leave his father and mother, and shall be joined to his wife: and they shall be one flesh (Gen. 2:18, 21–24).

The family is thus not incidental, but central, for from it comes all other human institutions.

The family constitutes the first church. Adam and Eve walked with God "in the cool of the evening." From the tents of the patriarchs and matriarchs arose Israel. To be a priest in the "church of the wilderness" was to be a member of the family of Levi. The New Testament church met for the most part in homes. In the missionary journeys of Paul, families were often the founding points of churches.

The family is also the focus of the first business enterprises. Patriarchal family groups and tribalities were economic structures that ensured survival. The term "economics" comes in fact from a Greek root meaning "the law of the household." Bedouin tribesmen can still be seen in countries of the Middle East; these herders and weavers make a living for the family whereby each member of the household contributes one's effort and expertise to a collective economic enterprise. In pioneer America and in the immigrant quarters of burgeoning cities, families worked together to ensure financial viability.

The family comprised the first state. The father and mother were figures of and for authority. In later European history, kings, queens, and princes considered themselves part of a family, whether or not a blood tie existed, and would address each other as "brother" and "cousin." During the Elizabethan era, the English queen was known as "the Mother of the Nation." A monument that overlooks the entire town of Coburg, Germany, commemorates a venerable prince and states that he was "a father of his people." A contemporary work of art depicts the primordial couple in Eden wearing crowns and ruling over the animals. This is in keeping with the biblical understanding of an embryonic state existing within the family.

The family was the context of the first school. The most important lessons of life, like speech, walking, sharing, and taking responsibility, are learned in the home. The family provided the initial education for some of our most outstanding luminaries. It was in the home that Augustine first heard of the mysteries of faith from Monica; that Basil read the classics of antiquity; that Bernard received training in rhetoric; that John Wesley first encountered the languages of the Scriptures; and it was probably there that Francis of Assisi first heard and was taught the poetry of Provence by Mona Pica. For all subsequent institutions, the home is not merely incidental, but central, for in it is found the formative nuclei of all social structures.

Because of its formative and informative qualities, the family is not transitional. It is not simply one phase of the human experience, eventually to be replaced by something else. It may be true that the family changes its form, like the extended family of former times or the nuclear and single-parent families of today; but in spite of changing times, the concept of the family unit remains the norm.

Francis recognized that the family is not simply biological, for more than biology is involved. There is, of course, a sexual basis for marriage and family. The medieval church insisted on consummation as part of a legitimate marriage, but marriage and the resultant family are not based on sex alone. Sex was to be an expression of intentional love, a willful choice, and a factor in a mutuality that included the heart, the mind, and the spirit. Most of those who joined Francis' Third Order were not celibate. They were men and women in families who allowed their love to be spread beyond the confines of their own home. The love of man and woman consummated in a marriage was to be expressed sociologically.

When Francis founded the intentional family of the Franciscan orders, he illustrated what makes a biological family work—mutual trust, loyalty, and submission. All of these result from the intention to love another in both word and deed. Love is the basis of the family, and Francis understood love.

2. The family is an affectional community. Like medieval theologians, Francis recognized that marriage and family are volitional, not compulsory. However, the "good will" prerequisite to the covenant of marriage and the commitment of parenthood is born of deep affection. The family on earth is to be patterned after the family in heaven, where God is the loving Father, Jesus is the beloved Son, and the Holy Spirit is the bond of uniting love.

The intimacy that exists within the Trinity is intended to characterize all forms of the Christian community. John, "the beloved disciple," wrote:

> Beloved, let us love one another: for love is God: and every one that loves is born of God, and knows God. He that loves not knows not God; for God is love (1 John 4:7–8).

The apostle Paul, in the same letter in which he gives an extended discussion of family life (cf. 1 Cor. 7), exults love, stating:

> And now abides faith, hope, love, these three: but the greatest of these is love (1 Cor. 13:13).

Peter, who was married, compared church and family, both affectional associations, saying,

> Be of one mind, having compassion for another, as family, be concerned, be courteous. . . . (1 Peter 3:8).

Love was the identifying mark of early Christianity. A pagan writer remarked, "Behold, how these Christians love one another."

Francis of Assisi was an apostolic Christian, even though he lived in the thirteenth century. His was the spirit of affection and charity that had characterized John, Paul, and Peter. One who knew Francis wrote:

> Since the strength of Francis' love made him a brother to all other creatures, it is not surprising that the charity of Christ made him more than a brother to those who were stamped with the image of their creator. . . . He did not consider himself a friend of Christ unless he loved the souls that Christ loved. . . . He loved his brothers beyond measure with an affection that rose from his innermost being, because they were of the same "household of faith" and united by participation in "an eternal inheritance according to the promise."[3]

This writer continued in another connection:

> St. Francis, exhorting all moreover to charity, admonished them
> to show to one another affability and the friendliness of family life.
> "I wish," he said, "that my brothers would show themselves to be
> the children of the same mother and that if anyone asks for a tunic
> or a cord or anything else, the other should give it to him with
> generosity. Let them share their books and anything else that is
> agreeable, so much so that one would even force the other to take
> it." And lest in this matter he should speak anything of those
> things Christ was not working through him, he was the first to do
> all these things.[4]

As Francis founded his order on the biblical model of the family,
so the Franciscan ethic of the family can be inferred from the affection
that existed in the order. The love that prevailed within the Franciscan
community was neither sexual or social; it was spiritual. It arose out of
a common commitment to Christ—a volitional choice to love others
as Christ loved them. This is also the ethos of the Christian home.

Marriage and family seek to unite in one community those who
are profoundly different: male and female, child and adult, young and
old. Those who form a family differ in age and generation, sex and
temperament, vocation and inclination. Biologically and psychologi-
cally the members of a family are not identical. In today's society racial
differences may also be present between the spouses or, through
adoption, between the parents and the children. With the breakup of
families and with remarriage following death or divorce, "blending" or
"mixing" of children from previous unions occurs. Diversity within the
family is increasing, not decreasing.

Society has conspired with nature to accentuate the variety that
may exist within the home. This means that the bond of Christian love
is needed more than ever. Neither sex nor friendship can suffice to
offer the transcendent and transforming power needed to meld into
one those who are inherently diverse. The Christ who could unite Jew
and Samaritan, Greek and barbarian, slave and freeman, male and
female, within the church can also provide "the bond of unity" for the
family. Thomas of Celano talked of the "binding and bonding" quality
of love exhibited by Francis:

> It was always Francis' anxious wish and careful watchfulness to
> preserve among his sons the bond of unity, so that those whom
> the same spirit drew together and the same father brought forth
> might be nurtured peacefully in the bosom of one mother. He
> wanted the greater to be joined to the lesser, the wise to be united

with the simple by brotherly affection, the distant to be bound to
the distant by the binding force of love.[5]

Many today both desire and fear this kind of love. They desire it,
for without it marriage may become mere cohabitation; with it,
marriage becomes an approximation of the love of God. They fear it,
because such intimacy with another entails a cost and the risk of loss.
Yet "sacramental union" cannot be had apart from a "sacrificial spirit."
This sentiment is suggested in many ancient Christian marriage
ceremonies. At one point in the rite of the Eastern Church, the priest
crowns the bride and groom, showing them to be king and queen,
inheritors of the promise of the Garden. Marriage is affirmed as the
sole surviving vestige of Eden, where God himself presided at the
wedding.

Yet Christian nuptials occur within the shadow of the Cross.
That cross, be it on altar or chancel wall, constantly testifies to the
sacrificial cost of love. A marriage begun in joyful celebration may lead
to sorrowful affliction. Many problems may appear. The couple may
find themselves, like Bunyan's pilgrim, bearing grievous loads and
battling giants in the course of their journeying together. Be it cross or
crown, however, Christ can be near. He is the one, seated with the
Father, who has a diadem on his head, yet the marks of the Tree still
upon his body. He is present, with love to fulfill—so that affliction
becomes benediction, and affection becomes joy eternal.

The State

> To all magistrates and counsuls, to all judges and all governors
> throughout the whole world and to all others who receive this
> letter, Brother Francis, your poor and contemptible servant in the
> Lord God, sends you greetings and peace.
> Consider and realize, that the "day of death is approaching." I
> beg you, therefore, with all the reverence I am capable of, that you
> do not allow all the cares and anxieties of the world you carry to
> let you forget God or turn from obeying his commandments. For
> all who forget him and "swerve from his commandments" "shall
> be forgotten by him." When the day of death comes, all that
> which you thought to possess "will be taken away." And those
> who were the greatest in wisdom and power in this life will be
> those who suffer the greatest torments in hell.
> And so, my lords, this is my counsel. Put aside all cares and
> anxiety and reverently receive the holy Body and holy Blood of
> our Lord Jesus Christ in holy memory of him.[6]

The overriding reality in the life of our contemporaries is the state. Our identity, unlike that of Francis of Assisi, is based to a significant degree on nationality. We are Germans, Americans, Britons, or Mexicans. Most identify themselves in terms of a country, not a city. Our prosperity, unlike that of "the Little Poor One," is based on membership in an industrial community. The state incorporates and regulates industry for economic activity. It can appropriate the financial resources of institutions and individuals.

Our security, unlike that of the medieval friar, does not depend on a feudal levy, a German emperor, or a town militia. We depend for protection from enemies, at home and abroad, on complex military, police, and intelligence services. Our equity, or justice, unlike that of "the Holy Vagabond," depends not on the courts of counts and kings, bishops and merchants, but on an intricate system of national and local judicial jurisdictions. Our destiny, unlike that of "the Troubadour," is not simply a matter of personal choice; it is quite often the result of public policy. Since the eighteenth century, the state has become an overwhelming reality for contemporary men and women. Without it civilization as we know it would cease to function. Our life is unintelligible without an appreciation of the role of the state.

Given this situation, it may seem very strange to quote Francis of Assisi in that connection. Most medieval persons were illiterate. Paper was scarce. Communication was often the result of chance rather than planning. Most people of that time were born, lived out their lives, and died in the same locale. Individuals depended on local personalities for their identity, security, prosperity, equity, and destiny. One's identity was derived from town, trade, family, or personal traits. One's security was a matter of local importance. The town militia protected the citizenry; the feudal lord and his levy defended the peasantry. One's prosperity was a matter of self-reliance, depending on the productivity of the serf in the manor field, the ability of the craftsman in the shop, or the discernment of the merchant at the fair. One's rights were established in local tribunals of various types—the bishop's court, the feudal court, the merchant court. There equity was established.

Destiny depended on decisions made at the lowest, not the highest, levels of society. Baron or master, mayor or bishop often decided the fate of the subject or apprentice, citizen or believer. The higher authority of pope and emperor could as often be ignored as it was obeyed. Into this environment came Francis—identified as a citizen of Assisi, a member of the town's militia, the son of a merchant, whose fate was decided in an episcopal court, who embraced the religious life—a choice that would strike some moderns as strange. In almost every respect Francis appears profoundly medieval, the antetype of most things contemporary.

While Francis is, of course, an intensely medieval personage, he is at the same time strikingly relevant to the realities of the twentieth century. An American biographer said of Francis, "he heralded the Renaissance." By this is meant that Francis embodied traits that have come to characterize contemporary men and women. No where is this more evident than in his posture toward the state. In his *Letter to the Rulers of the People,* Francis suggests five ways in which the Christian "renders unto Caesar the things that are Caesar's" and "unto Christ the things that are Christ's."

1. There is the matter of identity. Identity is in part determined by membership in civil communities. We speak of Jesus of Nazareth and Paul of Tarsus, both Israelites, both subjects of Caesar, both obedient to God. When the name Francis comes to mind, it is immediately followed by the identifying phrase "of Assisi." Francis was also an Italian, a subject of both pope and emperor in his time. Francis, however, like Jesus and Paul, recognized that one's identity was larger than one's membership in any society. In his *Letter to the Rulers* Francis indicates how he is able to reconcile his concurrent membership in two kingdoms—that of Caesar and that of Christ:

> To all magistrates and counsuls, to all judges and all governors throughout the whole world and to all others who receive this letter, Brother Francis, your poor and contemptible servant in the Lord God, sends you greetings and peace.[7]

This salutation, reminiscent of the fashion in which St. Paul began his letters, suggests the dialectical tension that Francis felt to be necessary for Christian life in the world. On the one hand, Francis has a profound respect for secular authorities; on the other, he includes all persons in his greeting, not simply princes, and he relates himself to both by regarding himself the servant of all in the name of God. In such a manner Francis reconciles the particular and the universal, both local authority and jurisdictions of wider scope. This tension, which pitted counts against emperors and emperors against popes, is, for Francis, dissolved into a network of intermeshing loyalties and opportunities for service. Francis also reconciles the earthly and the heavenly, the dual citizenship of the children of God: subject to secular authority, subject to heavenly calling. Our service to God provides our absolute identity; our service to others, our relative loyalty.

2. There is the matter of security. Security is in part determined by membership in a civil community. The apostle Paul appealed to Roman courts, was protected by imperial troops, and was tried before Caesar. Yet Paul was also a man of liberty who celebrated Christian freedom and refused conformity to ideas, individuals, and institutions that contradicted Christ. For Paul the state was to provide the necessary security to enable persons to serve their God according to conscience. Francis understood this ethic. In writing to the rulers of Europe, he advised: "Make sure that God is held in great honor among your subjects. . . . if you fail to have this done, be sure that you will render an account to our Lord Jesus Christ."[8]

Like Paul, Francis ministered within the framework of secular and ecclesiastical "security systems." His order flourished because of the protection of the papacy. Francis was able to witness to the Muslims because he followed a Crusader army to Egypt. Friars functioned under the jurisdiction of bishops in outlying regions. But like Paul, Francis was an "obedient rebel" who, when it was necessary, forfeited security for a greater liberty to serve Christ. To follow Jesus, Francis forsook the safety of his father's house, the predictability of a secular career, the regularity of married life, and the certainties of town life in Assisi. Rather than join an established order, Francis chose a mendicant life in which, like Paul, he wandered about the land. Like the apostle, Francis was beaten, robbed, shipwrecked, betrayed by false friends, misunderstood by superiors, and often forsaken by his peers. He knew cold and hunger, pain and lack of shelter. Yet, like Paul, he counted "all things loss" for the excellency of Christ.

3. There is the matter of prosperity. Prosperity is in part determined by membership in a civil community. Jesus was a carpenter, Paul a tentmaker. Francis encouraged the friars to work. Labor was dignified by the monastic communities. Francis exhorted the brothers to "labor with their own hands." Yet Francis believed that economic prosperity was not necessarily coterminous with spiritual well-being. Possessions could, in fact, cause one to perish. Francis wrote to magistrates:

> I beg you, therefore, with all the reverence I am capable of, that you do not allow all the cares and anxieties of the world you carry, to let you forget God or turn from obeying his command-

ments. . . . when the day of death comes, all that which you thought to possess "will be taken away."[9]

Jesus condemned the "wise fool" who built "bigger barns" while losing his soul. Paul forsook position and possessions, advising against covetousness. Francis testified to the affluent townsmen of his time through the witness of radical poverty. He spoke to a church that was steeped in riches, to a hierarchy accustomed to comfort, to states obsessed with wealth, to citizens grasping for luxuries. To his own friars Francis wrote, "Let poverty be your party." They were to "pass through this world as pilgrims and foreigners." From this we learn that Francis saw the furniture of fortune not as something inherently evil, but capable, like all else, of being used for either idolatry or ministry.

4. There is the matter of equity. Justice is in large measure a result of one's membership in a civil community. From the Code of Hammurabi to the United Nations Charter, human rights have been a major civilized concern. Moses gave his people Covenant and Commandments. Amos and the prophets of Israel proclaimed justice. Jesus inaugurated his ministry with the Sermon on the Mount, establishing a code based on a new commandment of love.

Francis, as one shaped by the Scriptures, appreciated the biblical emphasis on equity. In writing to the magistrates Francis said: "All who forget God and swerve from his commandments shall be forgotten by Him."[10] In this sentence Francis recognized the tension that can arise between the statutes of society and the imperatives of God.

Often the laws of the land and the duties of a Christian correspond. At times, however, grave disparities may exist. The state may command what is wrong or neglect to do what is right. Furthermore, judges cannot inspire those mental and moral qualities that are given by the Spirit of God and which are part of the very essence of justice. Like the Hebrew prophets, Francis could both preach in the court and yet protest from the wilderness. Sometimes he was like Nathan, at other times Amos. Always in the forefront of his thinking was the ultimate justice that God will bring at the *eschaton*. By it all other measures of righteousness are valued. When Christ judges the nations, the standard will be that of his kingdom, not the relative cultures of history. The basis for this judgment will be "whatsoever you have done to the least of these my brethren."

5. There is the matter of destiny. One's biography is in part

determined by the social and political environment in which one lives. Joseph went from slavery to mastery. Jeremiah went from freedom to servitude. David went from obscurity to celebrity. Paul went from fame as a Pharisee to apparent infamy as a teacher of the new sect called "Those of the Way." While the context of their careers must be considered, it is not in the final analysis the one crucial consideration. God is our ultimate destiny; all else is penultimate.

This is why Francis in writing to the most powerful men of his day said: "Consider and realize that the day of death is approaching. . . . those who were the greatest in wisdom and power in this life, will be those who suffer the greatest torment in hell."[11] Francis very likely recalled the sad saga of Saul, the wretched career of Jezebel, and the ignominious end of Herod. Conversely, he knew the honor given to the heroes of faith, who without accolades in this life received immortal glory from God.

The state cannot claim to exhaust all the potential of its people. Our destiny as Christians is not coterminous with Jerusalem, Rome, Constantinople, Moscow, London, or Washington. A person who has freedom in Christ is also freed from the ultimate end of the society in which he or she lives. Rome collapsed, but Augustine continued. Germany was in flames, but Dietrich Bonhoeffer left "a good report." The claims of pope and emperor in thirteenth-century Italy are discussed and debated by historians, but ignored by most people. Francis, however, has obtained immortality in history and eternity because, like Christ, he knew that the state and all it possesses is still not enough to be the fit price of a single human soul.

In each era of history Christians have been confronted with the claims of the state. The church has existed in its pilgrimage through time under monarchies and republics, dictatorships and empires, democracies and theocracies. As a result, much confusion has arisen in Christian thinking about "civil order." For this reason some suggest that the lesson to be learned from the life of Francis is that the state is to be ignored. One should act as if it is not. That seems simply to compound the confusion. Furthermore, it presents us with a caricature of Francis.

Francis of Assisi, we feel, was one so committed in love to God and humanity that he ministered within the confines of the state, not because the state itself was absolute, but because it was a creation of God designed to serve the needs of humanity. His message was one of liberation of the oppressed and confrontation of the oppressors.

Although he recognized the reality and the power of the state, he also realized that his ultimate loyalty belonged to God alone.

The Academy

> It is agreeable to me that you should teach the friars sacred theology, so long as they do not extinguish the spirit of prayer and devotedness over this study.[12]

Relating Francis and the academy immediately poses another paradox, an apparent contradiction. On the one hand, Francis was not a scholar. No one would confuse Francis with St. Thomas Aquinas, "the Angelic Doctor," teacher, writer of the *Summa Theologica,* and adviser to three popes. Nor would one confuse him with another contemporary, St. Dominic de Guzman, "the Watchdog of the Lord" and defender of the faith. Jacques de Vitry described Francis as "a simple and unlettered man, but pleasant and dear to God." On the other hand, Franciscans have been scholars. Many followers of Francis have made intellectual history—Duns Scotus, William of Occam, St. Bonaventure, Alexander of Hales, and Roger Bacon. Since the thirteenth century there has been a long and noble tradition of Franciscan scholarship, exemplified in the United States alone by more than twenty Franciscan colleges. How are we to resolve the paradox?

A clue has been provided by a professor at the University of Lyons who said, "It is not the function of the Christian Church to create a new civilization; it is the church's function to create the creators of a new civilization." That is what Francis did. As a renewer of the church, Francis, in the words of historian Will Durant, "reinvigorated Christianity by bringing back into it the spirit of Christ." A reformer rather than an educator, Francis nevertheless provided the prerequisites of scholarship and vision. The Old Testament reminds us, "Where there is no vision, the people perish" (Prov. 29:18). By inference, where there is vision, the people prosper.

Through his gift of vision Francis was able to facilitate scholarship in five ways.

1. Francis had a vision of the unity of nature. This provided a necessary prerequisite for the physical and life sciences, for it facilitated an understanding of our world as a *uni*verse, not a *multi*verse.

Francis perceived the world community. Paul Gallico, writing about "St. Francis and the Animals," noted that

> Francis had a relationship to everything: to man, beasts of the fields and forests, the birds, the fish, trees, flowers, even stones, the sun, the moon, the wind and the stars, fire and water, rain and snow, storms, the earth, summer, winter, and the tender elegy of springtime. With all of these he dealt courteously and admitted them to the circle of his immediate family.[13]

Through love Francis arrived at the capacity for harmony with nature. Francis practiced what Dr. Albert Schweitzer called "reverence for life." Love of nature is part of the biblical tradition. Adam was placed in a garden. Noah filled his ark with animals. Isaiah foresaw the messianic kingdom as a place where lion and lamb lie together. Christ is born in a manger "where ox and ass are feeding." Jesus referred to the lilies of the field, the sparrows of the air. Francis embodied that tradition. That is why he is said to have conversed with the wolf of Gubbio and the swallows are said to have refrained from singing while he preached. No wonder Francis sang of burning sun, silver moon, rushing wind, clouds that sail, flowing water, fire so masterful, mother earth, flowers and fruits, all men of tender heart, and kind and gentle death. Francis loved nature because he loved nature's God.

Theologian Paul Tillich once suggested that nature was conquered simultaneously in Greece and Israel—once by reason, once by love. The wisdom of the philosophers and the love of the prophets made it possible for persons to investigate and to appreciate nature.

Prior to such a revolution of attitudes, nature could not be known. For some, nature was to be feared, for it was demonic. For others, it was to be bribed, for it was capricious and unpredictable. For yet others, it was to be adored, for it was divine. For still others, it was to be destroyed, for it was an enemy. To all polytheists, nature was confusing, for it was a complex of contradictory energies.

Since the revolution of Greek philosophy and biblical religion, nature is a *cosmos,* a creation, an expression of a Supreme Intelligence. For Francis, as for the biblical prophets, nature was a trysting point of personality with personality. It is not strange that science flourished following the Franciscan revival, or that Roger Bacon, a Franciscan friar, was also a pioneering scientist. By intuition and affection Francis arrived at a vision of the unity of nature and predicated its rationality and intelligibility.

2. Francis had a vision of the solidarity of the human family. This provided a prerequisite for history and the social sciences, because it facilitated an understanding of our society as unity amid diversity.

One is impressed with the wide appeal of Francis of Assisi. A person of great and good reputation, he was quickly canonized by Pope Gregory IX in 1228, which was only two years after he died. He was recognized by his contemporaries and honored by posterity. All manner of Christians have been attracted to him. Francis remains a force among Roman Catholics, whether traditionalists or liberationists. Concurrently many types of Protestants have been attracted to him—men as varied as Paul Sabatier, a classic liberal; John Wesley, an Evangelical; and John Henry Newman, an Anglican who converted to Roman Catholicism. Moreover, the power of Francis has extended beyond the Christian community. Both Jews and Muslims honor him. A favorite figure of the counterculture of the 1960s, Francis was venerated for his emphasis on peace, simplicity, and charity.

Through love Francis has come to appeal to people of divergent backgrounds. He embodied the "new commandment" of Christ, "that you love one another, as I have loved you" (John 15:12). For that reason nothing human was alien to Francis. Noting this trait, Constantine Koser wrote:

> Francis encounters all men in God and lists them by categories, which themselves give eloquent testimony to the breadth of his love: "all children, big and small, the poor and needy, kings and princes, laborers and farmers, servants and masters, . . . all virgins and other women, married and unmarried, . . . all layfolk, men and women, infants and adolescents, young and old, the healthy and the sick, the little and the great, all peoples, tribes, families, and languages, all nations and men everywhere, present and to come."[14]

Francis recaptured the Christian vision of humanity as one family.

Daniel Luther Evans, a professor of philosophy at the Ohio State University, once observed: "Prior to the rise of Greek philosophy and Hebrew religion it was difficult to think in terms of 'humanity.' After their success and synthesis in the Catholic faith, it is impossible not to think in terms of 'humanity.'" By this Evans meant that before the Christian Era, people identified themselves by tribe, by city, by country, or some other peculiarity. After the birth of Christianity people saw themselves as common citizens of one kingdom that filled the earth. Men and women of all cultures, colors, classes, and conditions could image God in Christ and receive his Spirit. Francis rediscovered that sense of humanity.

It is not strange that the social sciences flourished following the

Franciscan revival. "The Little Poor One's" vision of the unity of humanity in spite of diversity provided a philosophical foundation for such studies. Scholar Page Smith has suggested that the dilemma facing the historian is that, on the one hand, time must make a difference, for we measure change; on the other hand, humanity must remain constant, else we could not comprehend our forebears. A similar dilemma faces the sociologist. Cultures must differ, else there is no point in contrasting them. Cultures must be similar, else there would be no basis of comparison. Through love Francis found the key, namely, that we, though many, are also one.

3. Francis had a vision of the capacity to communicate. This provided a prerequisite for the arts and humanities, for it facilitated an understanding of human personality.

Humans create and communicate. This is the testimony of history. Remains as far removed as the Temple of the Sun in Mexico, the pyramids of Giza in Egypt, and the illustrated cave of Lascaux in France bear witness to this truth. We are artists.

Humans create and communicate. This is the testimony of philosophy. Learned discourse was the mark of the civilized man in Greece, the polished sage in China, and the astute statesman in Britain. Rhetoric was a major contribution of the classical world to human civilization. We are wordsmiths.

Humans create and communicate. This is the testimony of Christian theology. The church originated among a people with a long oral tradition; it was born in preaching and preserved in Scripture. No wonder Muslims call Christians "People of the Book." We understand humankind as made in the image of God's child, called "the Word." We are poets like David, orators like St. Peter, songsters like St. Mary, and authors like St. Paul.

Francis was a communicator in words. Embracing the language of the people, Francis endowed it with vitality and beauty. Through his sermons and poems, songs and letters, testaments and admonitions, Francis, as has been stated above, helped create the Italian vernacular, the *dolce stil nuovo*. It is no wonder that the Franciscan revival was followed by a literary Renaissance.

Francis was also a communicator in deeds. Who can forget his action of embracing the leper? By his actions Francis inspired artists, including the immortal Giotto. Painters and sculptors pioneered new techniques in order to capture the genius of the Franciscan revival. It is no wonder that it was followed by an artistic Renaissance.

Some have suggested that the secret of Francis' skill in communication was his wit. While visiting Egypt, Francis was invited to speak before the sultan Melik el-Kamil. Summoning Francis and one of the brethren, the sultan decided to test them by placing at his door a carpet embroidered with crosses. The two Christians would have to

> tread upon their sacred symbol—which St. Francis did without the least hesitation. "Gracious me!" jeered the sultan. "So you trample on the Cross of Christ!" "Do you not know," replied Francis, "that on Calvary there were three crosses, one for Christ and two for the thieves? We adore the one; you can have the other two, and if you care to strew them on the ground why should we hesitate to trample on them?"[15]

While his wit was great, Francis' love was greater. That love compelled him to be among the Muslims to communicate the love of Christ in a time of war.

4. Francis had a vision of the need for ministry to persons in need. This provided a prerequisite for all the serving professions—education, medicine, law, business, and theology—because it facilitated an understanding of the aim and end of learning. Information is to be married to ministration. The noblest end of learning is serving one's neighbor.

That is the message of the biblical tradition. Although addressed as "rabbi" or "teacher," Jesus took the title of "servant." By so doing he connected study and service forever. Christ came "not to be ministered to, but to minister, and to give his life as a ransom for many" (Matt. 20:28).

Filled with love, Francis rediscovered the ethic of the Cross. Pope Pius IX called him "the most perfect image of our Lord that ever lived." That discovery came in stages. It started with the rebuilding of the Church of San Damiano. It concluded with the reception of the stigmata of Christ. Historian Henri Daniel-Rops described the incident as follows:

> In September 1224 he [Francis] climbed Alverno, amid the glory of sunlight and birdsong. On the morning of the 17th, after days of burning prayer that was a veritable anguish of love, suddenly, in that blinding ecstasy, he beheld a seraph flying with six wings and bearing in its supernatural form the image of the Crucified. How long did the vision last? What was the visionary's experience? We do not know. But on returning to his senses, he found himself bathed in agony—pain yet exquisite; for imprinted in his hands and feet and side were the wounds of our Lord's sacred

Passion, bleeding. The witness of Jesus Christ now bore in his own flesh the stigmata of his God.[16]

What all the story may mean, we do not know. But this one thing is clear: we are called to a cruciform life. That means being willing to be vulnerable for the sake of the sister or the brother. In the process we may be wounded, even for doing what is right. Like Rubashov, the hero in Arthur Koestler's novel *Darkness at Noon,* we ask:

> Must one also pay for deeds which were right and necessary? . . . Must one also pay for righteous acts? Was there another measure beside that of reason?
> Did the righteous man perhaps carry the heaviest debt when weighed by this other measure? Was his debt, perhaps, counted double—for the others knew not what they did?
> Did the righteous man perhaps carry the heaviest debt?[17]

We are often wounded for doing what is right. Like Francis, each of us in our own way will come to bear the marks of the cross. These stripes, however, become sources of healing; broken, we give wholeness to others. Sacrificial love was the vision of Francis. It is not strange that humanitarian services, such as care for the aged and the infirm, flourished during and following the Franciscan revival. Francis, who embraced suffering and found himself healed, provided the model for countless thousands who would follow. Through love Francis found the key in ministering to human need.

"Come and Follow Me"

One day Jesus was met along the way by a rich young ruler. "Good Master," he asked, "what good thing shall I do, that I may have eternal life?" (Matt. 19:15). Jesus summed up for him the commandments. "All these things have I kept from my youth up: what lack I yet?" (Matt. 19:20). Jesus, loving him, said, "If you will be perfect, go and sell what you have, and give to the poor, and you shall have treasure in heaven: and come and follow me" (Matt. 19:21).

That is a hard saying of Christ. It is hard for those in a family, in a modern state, or in a university, because in a real sense it is addressed not merely to a young man of the first century, but to everyone who has heard Christ's voice. Each will respond differently. Charles Williams, the Anglican author, observed that there will always be some who will interpret the saying literally; for them the *rejection* of the world is required. Likewise, there will always be more who will interpret the saying figuratively; for them the *reception* of the world is required. Either way we are to seek to serve humanity and to glorify God in the life of our present society, be it well or ill.

Destiny

I bid you goodbye, all you my sons, in the fear of God. Remain in him always. There will be trials and temptations in the future, and it is well for those who persevere in the life they have undertaken. I am on my way to God, and I commend you all to his favor.[1]

A best-selling novel of the early 1980s was *The Clowns of God* by Morris West. In this story a pope is deposed for predicting the imminent return of Christ. The pontiff has been led to anticipate the Parousia by the pressing problems of the late twentieth century—hunger, poverty, war, oppression, and racial injustice. All these seem to be beyond the capacity of any person or institution to resolve. It is as if with finite resources humankind has been asked to solve infinite problems. The only solution is apocalyptic, calling for divine intervention and a resolution of the global crisis.

Such a scenario is sobering. This could, indeed, be the millennial generation, and the end of all things could be within sight.

There is, however, a more sobering thought. What if there is no divine intervention through a termination of history? Suppose that instead of being a terminal generation we are called to be a transitional generation, commissioned by destiny to confront and solve these issues? This seems to be the contention of Arthur C. Clarke in *The*

118

Fountains of Paradise. In this novel Clarke compares the late twentieth century to "a time of troubles," the narrow mouth of a bottle through which the fluid of life must pass in order to give sustenance to future generations.

> This was what St. Francis did when he lay dying. . . . "My brothers," he said to the friars, "we must begin now to do something. Up to now we have done very little. . . . Christ's cross has the power to give a person new life, though the outward part of our nature is being worn down, our inner life is refreshed from day to day."[2]

Francis of Assisi, we believe, exemplifies virtues necessary for human survival. It is our purpose in this section to relate the saint of Assisi to six of the crucial issues confronting humanity in the late twentieth century. His philosophy is eminently relevant to the central issues of our times. This can be illustrated by reference to six paradoxes confronting our society today.[3]

Knowledge and Service

There is the paradox of knowledge and service. We believe that Francis of Assisi has something to say to this moral dilemma of the late twentieth century. Francis struggled with the problem of wisdom and love. He is a model of the sage who serves.

One of the startling lessons of Scripture is the fact that "the wisdom of man" is often regarded as "folly" in the eyes of God. The biblical witness condemns knowledge employed simply for self-satisfaction and self-aggrandizement. An incident related in the narrative of Christ's birth illustrates this. The same star that had been studied and had led the Magi from the East to Judea in order to worship the infant Jesus incited the wrath of Herod and certain of his scribes. The Magi brought gifts to sustain the child; Herod sent soldiers to destroy him. In the one instance information gained by diligent study was used for the preservation and exaltation of life; in the other it was employed for its destruction.

A startling fact about the Western world is that never before has the biblical passage been so fulfilled as now: "Many shall run back and forth, and knowledge shall be increased" (Dan. 12:4). The proliferation of information in our day is astonishing. We have reached the point where the combined knowledge of all humanity doubles with each decade. Satellites and shuttles circle the earth, submarines probe the depths of the seas, telescopes scan the infinities of the galaxies, and microscopes explore the intricacies of subatomic particles.

The wisdom God grants, however, must be matched with the love he proffers if humanity is truly to be served. Learning separated from a sense of ministry to humanity produces a sterile technology. We become remade in the image of the machine so that the nightmare of a planet of robots seems more like reality than the biblical picture of persons fashioned in the image of the Ultimate Personality.

Worse yet, the Garden can be, and has been, reduced to the Wilderness through the misapplication of technology by the "arts" of environmental destruction and ecological devastation. Deprivation of mind and spirit is as real as deprivation of resources to the millions who have been unable to sit at the table of learning at which the fate of the planet is decided. Illiteracy, superstition, cults and the occult, prejudice, and massive ignorance stand, oddly enough, alongside education as signs of this age. The century that produced the Holocaust is now able not only to contemplate the extermination of one people through incineration, but also to assure the total annihilation of the human family through thermonuclear war. These programs of mass destruction have been named, appropriately enough, M.A.D.—"Mutual Assured Destruction."

Francis of Assisi is a paradigm of what the Scriptures regard as a wise man, that is, "a fool for Christ's sake." Although born in an age of Scholasticism, when universities were being founded across Europe, Francis said, "It is not for us to be wise and calculating in the world's fashion; we should be guileless, lowly, and pure."[4] Apart from Christ, who is the Wisdom of God, knowledge is apt to be at best useless, at worst dangerous. Francis observed:

> They lack spiritual insight because the Son of God does not dwell in them, and it is he who is the true wisdom of the Father. It is of such men as these that the Scripture says, "their skill was swallowed up." They can see clearly and are well aware of what they are doing; they are fully conscious of the fact that they are doing evil, and knowingly lose their souls.[5]

For Francis, wisdom was born of adoration, grew through consecration and dedication, and led to ministration to those in need. Wisdom was a form of wealth to be given by those who possessed it to the children of the poor. The wise of each generation, like the Magi, must seek humanity's happiness and ultimate destiny, not merely in the physical sciences and humanities, but also in religious heritage and service to society.

Peace and Justice

There is the paradox of peace and justice. We believe that Francis of Assisi has something to say to this moral dilemma of the late twentieth century. Francis struggled with the problem of serenity and equity. He is a model of a preacher of righteousness.

One startling lesson of Scripture is that peace cannot be had apart from justice. Peace, as is implied in the biblical term *shalom,* is not a static condition, but an active process. Jesus, the Prince of Peace, had much to say about this. At the start of his ministry, in the Sermon on the Mount, he said, "Blessed are the peace*makers:* for they shall be called the children of God" (Matt. 5:9). At the conclusion of his ministry, confronting in Jerusalem a city that wanted serenity without equity, Christ said, "If you had known, even you, at least in this your day, the things which belong to your peace! But now they are hid from your eyes" (Matt. 19:42).

To those who practice oppression of the poor, the aged, the infirm, the sick and insane, minorities, and the defenseless, Jesus promises not peace but violence, for they have sown the seeds of hatred and will reap the harvest of death. This teaching of Christ was repeated by James the Elder, who saw in lust and greed the sources of war. "From what source come wars and fightings among you? Come they not from yourselves, even from your lusts that war in your members?" (James 4:1). Or again, as he rebuked the profiteers,

> Go to now, you rich men, weep and howl for your miseries that shall come upon you. . . .
> Behold, the hire of the laborers, who have harvested your fields, which is of you kept back by fraud cry: and the cries of them which have reaped are entered into the ears of the Lord of Sabaoth (James 5:4).

It is no accident that in the biblical record the Sabbath, the "day of rest and gladness," the "time of peace," was also a set time for the study of the Torah, God's law.

A startling fact about the Western world today is that never before in human history have so many millions been mobilized in an international peace movement; yet never before have so many been caught up in fear and violence. The late twentieth century is a time of confrontation—of black and white in South Africa, of Palestinian and Israeli in the Middle East. It is a time of class, racial, cultural, national, and economic confrontation. From Northern Ireland to Namibia, frustration levels are rising. In part the issue is political—lack of freedom. In part it is economic—lack of the wherewithal for a good life. Basically, however, the issue is spiritual—a divorce in contemporary thinking between peace and justice.

When the Great Powers met at Versailles in 1919 to bring peace to a war-torn planet, they thought it would be possible to guarantee tranquility for a generation through the humiliation, rather than the reconciliation, of Germany. Justice was denied the defeated, and compassion was withheld from the vanquished. The seeds of hate sown in the treaty were harvested in Poland and France a generation later. Even today we live with the consequences of the failures at Versailles and the later decisions of Yalta and Potsdam that built upon them.

Francis of Assisi is a paradigm of what the Scriptures regard as a preacher of righteousness. Like us, he lived in an era of confrontation. In the thirteenth century terrible urban riots swept Europe. Economic conflict occurred in the towns, pitting apprentice against master. Peasant violence took place in the countryside. It was the era of the Crusades, when violence was embraced by the church as an instrument of the kingdom of God. The Inquisition was soon to bring terror to the homes of many in Christendom. Into this context Francis came as an apostle of peace and justice, preaching reconciliation and restitution.

Francis was a peace*maker* because he was a person of righteousness, with the ability to inspire others to do good. He advised his followers:

> While you are proclaiming peace with your lips, be careful to have it even more fully in your heart. Nobody should be aroused to wrath or insult on your account. Everyone should rather be moved to peace, goodwill, and mercy as a result of your self-restraint.[6]

In another situation, Francis said:

> "Blessed are the peacemakers, for they shall be called the children of God." They are truly peacemakers who are able to preserve their peace of mind and heart for the love of our Lord Jesus Christ, despite all that they suffer in this world.[7]

For Francis, justice was centered in humanity having been created in the image of God. What we do to the least of our brothers and sisters we do to him. Peacemaking means restoring a network of right relationships to those who have been injured or deprived. Francis expressed this in going to those who were on the fringes of society, isolated by circumstances and prejudice from the rest of the community. It was for this reason that he embraced the outcasts and the poor. Christ also identified himself with the fringes of society. Jesus named as his disciples those who brought life and joy to the oppressed.

> Then shall the King say to them on his right hand, Come you blessed of my Father, inherit the kingdom prepared for you from the foundation of the world: For I was hungry, and you gave me meat: I was thirsty, and you gave me drink: I was a stranger, and you took me in: Naked, and you clothed me: I was sick, and you visited me: I was in prison, and you came to me. . . .
>
> Truly, I say to you, Inasmuch as you have done it to the least of these my brethren, you have done it to me (Matt. 25:34–36, 40).

This principle was so important to Francis that it was incorporated into his Rule for those who would seek to follow him.

> Be glad to live among social outcasts, among the poor and helpless, the sick and the lepers, and those who beg by the wayside. . . . remember our Lord Jesus Christ, the Son of the Living, All-powerful God. . . . he was poor and he had no home of his own.[8]

Production and Distribution

There is the paradox of production and distribution. We believe that Francis of Assisi has something to say to this moral dilemma of the late twentieth century. Francis struggled with the problem of privilege in an age of scarcity. He is a model of a compassionate steward.

A startling lesson of Scripture is that the privileged are more often than not the ones who stand under the judgment of God, and the oppressed are identified as those who bear the future. Not Pharaoh, but the Hebrew slaves received the covenant and grace; not the Pharisees, but the publicans and sinners were praised by Jesus and called to inherit the kingdom. This is a disturbing reality for the "fertile crescent" of the industrial world that stretches across the north temperate zone from Germany through Canada and the United States to Japan. In our brighter moments we like to identify ourselves with Moses; in our bleaker times we fear that we might be Ramses.

A generation ago Harry Emerson Fosdick, addressing a wealthy congregation in Riverside Church, New York City, spoke on "The Peril of Privilege." In that sermon Fosdick identified privilege as more than money or position, but instead regarded it as "a total cluster of acquired or inherited circumstances that set one apart from the majority of humankind."9 Such an extraordinary position can be dangerous, for it can cause us to have a confused identity. We cannot know ourselves because of the difficulty of separating self from either possessions or attainments. In addition to this, we can become insulated against the suffering of the world, isolated by education or income from ignorance or hardship. Privilege may commit us to the preservation of the status quo, rather than seeking creative and innovative solutions for oppressive situations.

It was for this reason that William Ewart Gladstone, a British statesman of the Victorian Age, said, "During the preceding half century the privileged classes, the aristocratic classes, the educated classes, have been on the wrong side of every great social issue, and if their opinion had prevailed, it would have been to the detriment, or even the ruin of the country." The solution to the problem of privilege is found in a renunciation of selfishness and in the dedication of gifts and resources for the service of the poor.

The plight of the Western world in general, and of the Catholic and Protestant churches in particular, is affluence. Never has so much been given to so few in times of such need. The steady spread of communism is a testimony, not to the truth of the Marxist diagnosis, but to the intensity of suffering in our world and the rising tide of human desperation.

Francis of Assisi is a paradigm of the privileged person released to serve others. Born into an upper-middle class family in a prosperous Italian city, destined for a career as a knight, Francis received a vision that set his priorities right. As Paul, the privileged Pharisee, became through a Damascus road experience a servant of the oppressed, so Francis through the message of Christ learned how to place education and natural ability in the service of the people.

One biblical example of such stewardship is the story of Joseph. Privileged by birth, separated from others by both physical and spiritual gifts, Joseph seemed destined for a sheltered life. God used adversity and hardship—slavery and imprisonment, exile and mistreatment—to turn Joseph into an administrator of much for the needs of many. Under his jurisdiction the wealth of Egypt was employed for the health of nations. It seems to us that in our generation God is issuing an invitation to the affluent "Joseph nations" of the West and North to become stewards of life to their "famishing brethren" from the East and South.

This kind of responsibility was recognized by Francis as one of great and solemn joy. He said:

> Whoever sets aside a poor man does an injury to Christ, whose noble image he wears, the image of him who made himself poor for us in this world.[10]

Ministry to those in need, whether persons or nations, is high and noble. As we approach the twenty-first century the seeds of both life and death have been planted in the soil of the planet. Sword and plowshare, grain silo and missile silo are all symbols of the alternatives that are ours. May we, like Francis and Joseph, choose life, not death, and live in service under grace and not perish in selfishness under wrath.

Tranquillity and Activity

There is the paradox of tranquillity and activity. We believe that Francis of Assisi has something to say to this moral dilemma of the late twentieth century. Francis struggled with the problem of prayer and labor. He is a model of a man of meditation and action.

One startling lesson of Scripture is that Jesus, seen as a man of action who went about doing good, always took time to pray. Although we frequently find Christ in the marketplace, the synagogue, or along the highway, we just as often discover him in the silence of the garden or the mountain, engaged in prayer.

For Christ, the sense of the later Latin slogan *ora et labora* ("pray and work") was a daily reality. This sentiment was continued in the life of the Christian church. Paul both founded congregations and was caught up to the third heaven. James was renowned for both his preaching and his life of prayer. The monks of the early Catholic tradition led a balanced life of devotion and exertion. The Benedictine Rule prescribed exercise for both the soul and the body, through meditation and action. Both parts of the human personality—the spiritual and the physical—were to be kept in harmony. It is the lesson of Scripture and tradition that this principle of alternation is to be practiced by all, for prayer and labor must be kept in a proper relationship.

One startling fact about the Western world today is that seldom before in human history has so much information been disseminated on the devotional life. Quakers like Rufus Jones and Elton Trueblood have shared with many the intimacies of "the life with God." Catholic mystics like Carlo Carretto have instructed the multitudes as to the life of liturgy and piety. Yet for millions of Christians, prayer is isolated from labor. Anxiety, not adoration, is a major trait of our time.

Francis of Assisi is a paradigm of the man of prayer at work in the world. By word and deed Francis commended a life to both the friars and the public that balanced piety and activity, prayer and labor.

> The friars to whom has been given the grace of working should work in a spirit of faith and devotion, and avoid idleness, which is the enemy of the soul, without, however, extinguishing the spirit of prayer and devotion, to which every temporal consideration must be subordinate.[11]

As he approached the hour of his death, Francis had become revered in his own generation as a man of great devotion. His prayers had already become the common property of the Italian people. Many venerated him as a living saint who constantly practiced the presence of Jesus in his daily life. Many were tempted to imitate Francis by fleeing the life of field and farm for that of chapel and choir. This profoundly disturbed Francis. On his deathbed Francis said, "I worked with my own hands and I am still determined to work; and with all my heart I want the other friars to be busy with some kind of work that can be carried on without scandal."[12]

Earlier in his career Francis had warned his followers against those who would become "professional religionists." He explained to them what true piety consists of.

> "Blessed are the poor in spirit, for theirs is the kingdom of heaven." There are many people who spend all their time at their prayers and other religious exercises and mortify themselves by long fasts and so on. But if anyone says as much as a word that implies a reflection on their self-esteem or takes something from them, they are immediately up in arms and annoyed. These people are not really poor in spirit. A person is really poor in spirit when he hates himself and loves those who strike him in the face.[13]

Francis, however, would probably admonish our century in a somewhat different fashion. To a generation of "workaholics," to people who seldom frequent the sanctuary and "the silent hour" that brings renewal, Francis, we believe, would encourage us to "come to the quiet." In the cloister of private prayer we receive forgiveness of sin, correction of faults, relief from guilt, and freedom from the burden of the past; thereby we receive opportunity and energy for new beginnings.

Francis reminds us that we are called to a cruciform life. When Jesus was nailed to the tree, he was engaged in both prayer and labor. The Carpenter, by whom the world was made, fashioned salvation for us on the cross; concurrently, Christ was our Priest on Golgotha, making intercession for us, rending the veil of the temple, and giving access for the many to the holy. Our living and dying, like his, must combine working and praying, action and meditation.

Liberty and Authority

There is the paradox of liberty and authority. We believe that Francis of Assisi has something to say to this moral dilemma of the late twentieth century. Francis struggled with the problem of freedom and order. He is a model of a prophet from the people.

One startling lesson of Scripture is that liberty and authority are interdependent. Moses the liberator is also Moses the lawgiver. David the freedom fighter is also David the king. Josiah the reformer is also Josiah the monarch. Christ the Deliverer is also Christ the Lord. Freedom cannot exist apart from order. Freedom without order is anarchy. Order without freedom is tyranny. Freedom together with order in proper harmony constitutes "the good society."

One startling fact about the world today is that never before in human history have so many millions aspired to freedom; yet never before have so many millions languished in bondage. For more than three centuries the Western world has known great revolutions: the British Revolution of 1688; the American Revolution of 1776; the French Revolution of 1789; and the Russian Revolution of 1917. These struggles for liberty have inspired similar revolutions in much of the non-Western world: in Latin America, starting with men like Simon Bolivar; in Africa south of the Sahara, where the cry was for *uhuru* ("freedom"); and throughout Asia, where under the guidance of

men like Sun Yat-sen and Gandhi the masses of China and India strove
to find sovereignty and national destiny.

Yet, in spite of the rise of revolutions around the world, with
many pronouncements about "independence" and "the rights of man,"
tyranny remains a haunting reality for much of the planet in the late
twentieth century. Revolution has often served as but a prelude to new
oppression. Many South American countries have undergone repeated
revolutions only to experience repeated and continual oppression. In
the wake of revolution and republic, Germany experienced Hitler;
Russia, Lenin and Stalin; Spain, Franco; and China, Mao Tse-tung.
Still other societies have simply lapsed into anarchy—a collapse almost
beyond comprehension, as in the case of the Congo in the 1960s. It
has been difficult in our time to balance liberty and authority.

Francis of Assisi is a paradigm of what it means to be a prophet
both from and to the people—like Moses proclaiming both freedom
and order. The French scholar Sabatier heralded Francis as a model
citizen and freeman in Christ. At first glance this opinion seems
incredible. Francis has been thought of by many as the archetypal
rebel. It was Francis who forsook the ways of war to become a knight
of Christ. It was Francis who sold his father's goods to feed the poor.
It was Francis, the son of a businessman, who embraced poverty and
denounced materialism. It was Francis who sought freedom from
parental control and set aside his father's name. It was Francis who
founded an order in which the freedom of brothers to wander, preach,
or retreat to hermitages was paramount. It was Francis who, toward
the end of his life, rejected the strictures placed on the order he had
founded. It was Francis who at his life's close welcomed Sister Death
as a liberator.

On further reflection, however, the mystery of the "model citizen
and freeman in Christ" is resolved in the dialectical tension of
obedience and freedom. While Francis forsook the military for a life of
pacifism, this action is not to be understood as something arbitrary or
anarchistic. It was instead the expression of a loyalty to a "higher law,"
for he had experienced a summons to a "new obedience." While
Francis forsook his father's house for a life of asceticism, this action is
not to be understood as an act of self-willed disobedience. It was the
manifestation of a love for a greater family: the people of God.

While Francis founded an order of brothers based on much
liberty, it must never be forgotten that the friars were subject to the
authority of the church. While Francis himself later rejected certain of

the rules that had been imposed by others on his brotherhood, he did so only in the spirit of Christ, who had given him the initial vision of what the order was to be. The reality had fallen short of the ideal and needed to be recalled to its initial purity.

Indeed, while Francis welcomed Death, it was in the name of Life—for to him the grave was but the anteroom to the court of the great King, whom he had been summoned to serve. Francis was an obedient rebel. As a prophet both from and to the people, who preached to both princes and peasants, the saint of Assisi could say, "Blessed that person who is just as unassuming among his subjects as he would be among his superiors."[14]

Self-Fulfillment and Self-Denial

There is a paradox of self-fulfillment and self-denial. We believe that Francis of Assisi has something to say to this moral dilemma of the late twentieth century. Francis struggled with the problems of success and sacrifice. He is a model of a good physician.

A startling lesson of Scripture is that success and sacrifice are both present as components of the abundant life. Jesus, for example, comes into history as the Healer, the mender of broken bodies and spirits who causes the blind to see, the lame to walk, the deaf to hear, the crippled to run, the lepers to be clean, and the dead to rise to life. Christ regarded physical, emotional, and spiritual afflictions as enemies. "The fullness of life" was something to be desired and implemented for his servants. Often, therefore, Jesus furnished the afflicted, with energy and recovery so that they could return to a renewed and fruitful life.

By contrast, however, Jesus called his disciples to be willing to take up the cross, to endure physical pain and social ostracism for his sake. Christ the Master Healer became the Wounded One of Golgotha. According to tradition, all his apostles save John died violent deaths. The biblical portrait of the saintly life is one of tension between self-fulfillment and self-denial, between "gaining" and "losing" one's life. Fortunate are they who, like St. Paul, know when they are to abound and when they are to be abased—and to find contentment in both.

One startling fact about the world today is that never before have so many millions sought self-fulfillment and so many millions found only involuntary sacrifice. On the one hand, in the affluent upper tier of the northern hemisphere the good life has come within the reach of many. This is not to deny the existence of poverty and ill-health in this region, but it is to affirm that many of the physical scourges of the past, which often impoverished, incapacitated, or killed have been banished. Cholera, diphtheria, polio, and the "great plagues" have virtually disappeared. A long and fruitful life is now attainable for many. With the physical basis for success secured, it has been possible for vast numbers of men and women to achieve personal, social, financial, and cultural fulfillment.

On the other hand, in our century billions in the non-Western world have experienced deprivation almost beyond belief. In the slums of Cairo and on the streets of Calcutta, in the *barrios* of Caracas and the *gecekondus* of Istanbul, millions live in perennial poor health, lacking the stamina and strength to escape the bondage of poverty. Life spans remain short. Epidemics are common. Prospects are grim. It is of little comfort to know that physicians trained for India or Egypt often practice in Sussex or California, that nurses educated for Kerala often end up in Kuwait. Nor is it easy to understand how the "pursuit of self-fulfillment" in the West has become an almost neurotic quest for temporal immortality, while the compulsory "self-denial"of the Third World has become a kind of "hell within history."

Francis of Assisi is a paradigm of what it means to be a good physician—one who is self-fulfilled through self-sacrifice. Like Jesus, Francis was a wounded healer who could experience joy even in the midst of pain because his self-sacrifice was for the sake of others. Before his death "the Little Poor One" recounted to his brothers how he began his pilgrimage.

> This is how God inspired me, Brother Francis, to embark upon a life of penance. When I was in sin, the sight of lepers nauseated me beyond measure; but then God himself led me into their company, and I had pity on them. When I had once become acquainted with them, what had previously nauseated me became a source of spiritual and physical consolation for me.[15]

Francis became, like Jesus, a healer of the sick. Thomas of Celano later wrote of this time in the saint of Assisi's life.

> Then the holy lover of complete humility [Francis] went to the lepers and lived with them, serving them most diligently for God's sake; and washing all foulness from them, he wiped away also the corruption of the ulcers.[16]

Although Francis had once sought success by acquiring possessions and achieving fame, he found true fulfillment in self-surrender, giving not merely of what he had but of what he was. That is why one who knew him well explained Francis as follows:

> He therefore resolved in his heart never in the future to refuse any one, if at all possible, who asked alms for the love of God. This he most diligently did and carried out, until he sacrificed himself entirely and in every way; and thus he became first a practicer before he became a teacher of the evangelical counsel: "To him who asks of thee" he said, "give; and from him who would borrow of thee, do not turn away."[17]

Franciscan insights can indeed speak to the issues of our time and prepare us as men and women for the century to come.

"I Have Done What Was Mine to Do"

Francis has the ability to draw all sorts of men and women to himself. The virtues that he exemplified have been repeated time and time again in the lives of countless other Christians—both well known and little known. The reason for this is found in the love of the Crucified. The gifts given to the eternal Son of God take on in some portion infinite and eternal significance. This is true whether the gift is of our substance or our person.

When Francis gave himself fully to Christ, his life took on an importance that transcends time, distance, denomination, and country. The call to a "Franciscan" life that embodies these insights has gone out to Methodists in America, Roman Catholics in Albania, Presbyterians in Japan, Lutherans in Germany, Orthodox in Russia, and Anglicans in Great Britain. Many have been drawn, some unknowingly, to imitate a man who walked closely with Christ. They have in turn taken his message of simplicity, peace, and joy to the four corners of the earth.

The call to such a life continues today. Such persons will not always imitate Francis in dress, demeanor, or particularity of faith, but they will seek to bring the same insights and the same message of love to the issues that will face them in their time and place. Francis said, as he laid dying, "I have done what was mine to do; may Christ teach you what you are to do."[18]

Bibliographic Essay

> Francis taught that the testimony of God should be sought in books, not precious ones; to find edification, not beauty. However, he wanted only a few to be had, such as would be suited to the needs of the poor brothers.[1]

There is an immense amount of information available concerning Francis of Assisi—much more than can be listed in these few pages. The following bibliographic entries are meant to be suggestive of the volumes available, and not exhaustive. We have limited ourselves to books that are readily at hand for English-speaking readers. There are many fine works in German, French, and Italian that have provided much help in our research. To list only some would be unfair to others; to list all in this short essay would be impossible.

Bibliographies

For the serious student, a number of fine bibliographies are available. The oldest of the ones we recommend is *A Guide to Franciscan Studies* (London: SPCK, 1920), compiled by Andrew G. Little. Though the book is dated, its topical format is helpful. More recent are *Francis of Assisi and His Spirit: A Bibliography of Modern English Works on the Five Themes of Franciscan Spirituality* (Cincinnati: St. Clare Convent, 1978); Irenaeus Herscher's *Franciscan Literature: A Preliminary Checklist* (St. Bonaventure, N.Y.: Franciscan Institute, 1952), which includes incunabula and rare books concerning Francis; and the most complete listing in English, the bibliographic appendix prepared by the noted scholar Raphael Brown for *An English Omnibus of Sources for the Life of St. Francis,* edited by Marion A. Habig, 3d ed. (Chicago: Franciscan Herald Press, 1977). Each of these works will provide an

132

abundance of reference material for the study of Francis and Franciscan spirituality.

History

There is a wealth of material about the historical setting in which Francis lived. One of the standard, though dated, comprehensive histories of the Middle Ages is the eight-volume *Cambridge Medieval History* (New York: Cambridge University Press, 1924), containing many excellent articles by leading scholars of the day. A one-volume history, now used as a text in many universities, is Norman F. Cantor, *Medieval History,* 2d ed. (New York: Macmillan, 1969). A short overview of the period with a delightful emphasis on Francis is provided by Christopher Brooke, *The Structure of Medieval Society* (New York: McGraw-Hill, 1978).

More detailed studies concerning relevant aspects of medieval history are S. R. Packard, *Europe and the Church Under Innocent III* (New York: Russell and Russell, 1968), covering the time in which Francis founded his order; J. Jungmann, *The Mass of the Roman Rite* (New York: Benziger, 1955), dealing with the medieval liturgy of the Roman church; R. Bretano, *The Two Churches* (Princeton: Princeton University Press, 1968), focusing on the ecclesiastical politics of the age; Norman F. Cantor, *The Meaning of the Middle Ages* (Boston: Allyn and Bacon, 1973), presenting a sociological analysis of the period; M. D. Chenu, *Nature, Man, and Society in the Twelfth Century* (Chicago: University of Chicago Press, 1968), examining the context into which Francis was born from an anthropological perspective. P. Dronke, *Medieval Latin and the Rise of the Love Lyric* (New York: Oxford University Press, 1966), provides a useful study of the predominant literature of the day; R. W. Southern, *The Making of the Middle Ages* (New Haven: Yale University Press, 1953) supplies an overall view of medieval culture in this book, which has become a classic; and J. K. Hyde, *Society and Politics in Medieval Italy* (New York: St. Martin's, 1973) is insightful as it focuses attention on the country of Francis' birth and ministry.

An understanding of the Crusading spirit that swept medieval Europe is found in the authoritative modern account of Sir Steven Runciman's three-volume *History of the Crusades* (New York: Harper & Row, 1955).

Biography

A volume that contains Francis' writings, several early biographies and legends, and an excellent reference section is the aforementioned *English Omnibus of Sources for the Life of St. Francis.* A better one-volume work cannot be found. Edited by Marion A. Habig, it contains the work of a number of noted Franciscan scholars and is equipped with concordances and indexes. A volume to use alongside the *Omnibus* is the *Workbook for Franciscan Studies: Companion Guide to the Omnibus of Sources* (Chicago: Franciscan Herald Press,

1979), prepared by Damien Isabell, OFM, of the Catholic Theological Union, Chicago.

There are a number of good, modern biographies of the saint of Assisi. We are including in this section works in English or translated into English that have achieved a certain measure of scholarly or popular acclaim.

The most up-to-date and comprehensive biography now on the market is the English edition of Arnaldo Fortini's *Francis of Assisi (Nova Vita Di San Francesco)*, translated by Helen Moak (New York: Crossroad, 1981). Fortini gives information to help in the understanding of each place and event in the life of Francis as well as excellent historical backgrounds. The most popular of recent biographies and perhaps the most accessible is Julien Green's *God's Fool: The Life of Francis of Assisi* (New York: Harper & Row, 1985). Other recommended biographies include a fictionalized version by Nikos Kazantzakis, *St. Francis: A Novel*, translated by P. A. Bien (New York: Simon and Schuster, 1962); the standard *St. Francis of Assisi* by the Danish scholar Johannes Jorgenson, translated by O'Conner Sloane (New York: Longmans, Green, 1912), now in its tenth reprinting; the classic *Saint Francis of Assisi* by G. K. Chesterton (New York: George H. Doran, 1924); the timeless *Life of St. Francis of Assisi* by the French liberal Protestant Paul Sabatier, translated by L. S. Houghton (New York: Scribner's, 1894), having gone through twenty-one reprints in English prior to 1944; a devotional life, *The Peace of St. Francis,* by Maria Sticco, translated by Salvator Attanasio (New York: Hawthorne, 1962); and Theodore Maynard's *Richest of the Poor: The Life of Saint Francis of Assisi* (New York: Doubleday, 1948).

Other biographical works of interest include T. S. R. Bosse, *St. Francis of Assisi* (Bloomington, Ind.: Indiana University Press, 1968); Edward Armstrong, *St. Francis: Nature Mystic* (Berkeley: University of California Press, 1973); N. G. van Doornick, *Francis of Assisi: A Prophet for Our Times,* translated from the Dutch by Barbara P. Fasting (Chicago: Franciscan Herald Press, 1978); Omer Englebert, *St. Francis of Assisi: A Biography,* translated from the French by Eve M. Cooper (Chicago: Franciscan Herald Press, 1965); Ephrem Longpre, *A Poor Man's Peace,* translated from the French by Paul Barrett (Chicago: Franciscan Herald Press, 1969); John R. H. Moorman, St. Francis of Assisi (London: SCM Press, 1950); Ray C. Petry, *Francis of Assisi: Apostle of Poverty* (Durham, N.C.: Duke University Press, 1941); and the "first person" biography by Carlo Carretto, *I, Francis* (Maryknoll, N.Y.: Orbis, 1982).

Community

The founding of the Friars Minor and the subsequent history of the orders that grew out of it have been treated in a number of good books. General histories of interest are Herbert Holzapfel, *The History of the Franciscan Order,* translated from the German by A. Tibesar and G. Brinkman (Teutopolis, Ill.: St. Joseph Seminary, 1948); Raphael M. Huber, *A Documented History of the Franciscan Order* (Milwaukee: Nowiny, 1944), incorporating a number of source materials; and a recent scholarly work by John R. H. Moorman, *A History of the Franciscan Order From Its Origins to the Year 1517* (Oxford: Clarendon Press, 1968). A very fine and readable study has been provided by Lazaro Iriarte in his *History of the Franciscan Order* (Chicago: Franciscan Herald Press, 1983).

For more specialized studies incorporating certain of the categories examined in this volume, we recommend Rosiland B. Brooke, *The Coming of the Friars* (New York: Barnes and Noble, 1975), covering the emergence of the Franciscans; and the definitive *Origins of the Franciscan Order* by Kajetan Esser, translated by A. Daly and I. Lynch (Chicago: Franciscan Herald Press, 1970). On the subject of missions, helpful information is found in Daniel E. Randolph, *The Franciscan Concept of Mission in the High Middle Ages* (Lexington: University Press of Kentucky, 1975), and another volume by Kajetan Esser, *The Order of St. Francis: Its Spirit and Mission in the Kingdom of God*, translated by I. Brady (Chicago: Franciscan Herald Press, 1959). Literature is treated in John V. Fleming, *An Introduction to the Franciscan Literature of the Middle Ages* (Chicago: Franciscan Herald Press, 1977), and David L. Jeffrey, *The Early English Lyric and Franciscan Spirituality* (Lincoln: University of Nebraska Press, 1975).

Spirituality

The spirituality of Francis of Assisi remains an inspiration and an enigma to interpreters of his life. Among the many volumes devoted to this subject, written from varying perspectives, we recommend two volumes by the noted Franciscan scholar Duane V. Lapsanki, *Evangelical Perfection* (St. Bonaventure, N.Y.: Franciscan Institute, 1977) and *The First Franciscans and the Gospel* (Chicago: Franciscan Herald Press, 1976); the important study by Leonardo Boff, *Saint Francis: A Model for Human Liberation* (New York: Crossroad, 1984); the intriguing monograph by Maurice F. Egan, *The Life of St. Francis and the Soul of Modern Man* (New Haven, Conn.: Yale University Press, 1983); the standard, *I Know Christ: The Personality and Spirituality of St. Francis of Assisi* by Gratien de Paris, translated by P. Oligny (St. Bonaventure, N.Y.: Franciscan Institute, 1957); the timeless *Ideals of St. Francis of Assisi*, translated by Berchmans Bittle (New York: Benziger, 1925); Cuthbert of Brighton, *The Romanticism of Saint Francis* (New York: Longmans, Green, 1924); Antonellus Engemann, *The New Song: Faith, Hope and Charity in Franciscan Spirituality*, translated by Isabel and Florence McHugh (Chicago: Franciscan Herald Press, 1964); Kajetan Esser, *Repair My House*, translated by Michael Meilach (Chicago: Franciscan Herald Press, 1977); Cesaire de Tours, *Franciscan Perfection*, translated by Paul Barrett (Westminister, Md.: Newman Press, 1956); Efrem Bettoni, *Nothing For Your Journey*, translated by Bruce

Malina (Chicago: Franciscan Herald Press, 1959); Valentin M. Breton, *Lady Poverty,* translated by Paul Oligny (Chicago: Franciscan Herald Press, 1963); Hilaron Felder, *The Ideals of St. Francis of Assisi* (Chicago: Franciscan Herald Press, 1983); and a specialized study concerning the life of prayer by Cornelia Jessey, *The Prayer of Cosa: Praying in the Way of Francis of Assisi* (New York: Harper & Row, 1985).

Notes

Abbreviations

1C   Thomas of Celano's *First Life of St. Francis*
2C   Thomas of Celano's *Second Life of St. Francis*
3S   *Legend of the Three Companions*
Fior.   *Fioretti, or Little Flowers of St. Francis*
LM   *Major Life of St. Francis* by St. Bonaventure
Lm   *Minor Life of St. Francis* by St. Bonaventure
Test.   *Testament of St. Francis*

Unless otherwise indicated all quotations from the works listed above, as well as the other writings of St. Francis and his early followers, are from the translations in *An English Omnibus of Sources for the Life of St. Francis,* ed. Marion A. Habig, 3d ed. (Chicago: Franciscan Herald Press, 1977), and are used by permission.

Introduction

1. St. Francis, *Rule of 1221,* 17.

One: Life

1. *Augsburg Confession,* article 7.
2. 2C, 3.
3. 3S, 2.
4. The most popular work that is concerned with this material is Erik H. Erikson, *Young Man Luther* (New York: W. H. Norton, 1962). The conclusions concerning Luther are at times exaggerated but are nonetheless thought provoking.
5. 3S, 2.

6. 3S, 4 and 2C, 4.

7. 3S, 8.

8. Cf. Richard Barber, *The Reign of Chivalry* (New York: St. Martin's, 1980), 15–16.

9. 2C, 6.

10. LM, 1.5.

11. LM, 2.1.

12. Ibid.

13. 3S, 20.

14. St. Jerome, *Commentaries on Isaias,* 14, 53, 5.

15. 1C, 22.

16. LM, 7.

17. LM, 3.

18. Cf. 2C, 17 and 3S, 51.

19. *Legend of Perugia* (*Omnibus* trans.), 114.

20. There is some discussion as to the actual date and year of the Chapter of Mats. In the present study the authors have given the traditionally assigned chronology. For other interpretations of this material, see Omer Englebert, *St. Francis of Assisi: A Biography,* trans. Eve M. Cooper (Chicago: Franciscan Herald Press, 1965), 189, note 2.

21. LM, 1.

Two: Meaning

Worship

1. St. Francis, *Letter to All Superiors of the Friars Minor.*

2. St. Francis, *Letter to All Clerics.*

3. Ibid.

4. Preparatory Rite, *The Service Book and Hymnal of the Lutheran Church in America* (Minneapolis: Fortress, 1958), 15.

5. Ignazio Silone, *Bread and Wine,* trans. Gwenda David and Eric Mosbacher (New York: Penguin, 1946), 320.

6. Carlo Carretto, *The God Who Comes,* trans. Rose Mary Hancock (Maryknoll, N.Y.: Orbis, 1974), 36.

7. Test.

8. St. Francis, *Letter to All the Faithful.*

9. "Enchiridion: The Small Catechism of Dr. Martin Luther," *The Book of Concord,* trans., ed. T. G. Tappert et al. (Philadelphia: Muhlenberg, 1959), 349.

10. St. Francis, *Rule of 1223,* 8.

11. St. Francis, *Letter to All the Faithful.*

12. St. Francis, *Rule of 1221,* 16.

13. Ibid., 23.

14. St. Francis, *Letter to All the Faithful.*

15. Ibid.

16. Henri Daniel-Rops, *Cathedral and Crusade,* trans. John Warrington (Garden City, N.Y.: Image, 1963), 80.

17. St. Francis, *Rule of 1221,* 9.

18. St. Francis, *Letter to Brother Leo.*

19. Murray Bodo, *Francis: The Journey and the Dream* (Cincinnati: St. Anthony Messenger, 1972), 168.

20. St. Francis, *The Praises Before the Office.*

21. St. Francis, *Letter to a General Chapter.*

Theology

1. St. Francis, *Praises of God,*

2. St. Francis, *Letter to All the Faithful.*

3. 1C, 2.

4. St. Francis, *Canticle of Brother Sun.*

5. Fior., 8. This particular version of the story of "perfect joy" was published in 1927 and follows a fourteenth-century Latin manuscript that differs considerably from the traditional version. Cf. *English Omnibus,* 1501.

6. 1C, 58.

7. Test.

8. Fior., 9.

9. Test.

10. 1C, 1.

11. ML, 4.

12. 1C, 73.

Society

1. St. Francis, *Letter to All the Faithful.*

2. St. Francis, *The Rule of the Third Order, 1221,* 18.

3. 2C, 172.

4. 2C, 180.

5. 2C, 191.

6. Translated by the authors from the Latin text of *Letter to the Rulers of the People,* edited by H. Boehmer and published in *Analekten zur geschichte des Franciscus von Assisi.* Although the origin of this letter was not always considered to be from the hand of St. Francis, more recent scholarship has argued for its authenticity. The text was included in Francis Gonzaga's work concerning the origins of the Franciscan Order which was published between 1579 and 1587. Gonzaga states that a copy of the letter was already in circulation by the year 1227 and was included in documents brought from Spain by John Parenti in c. 1228. The style of the letter certainly commends it as a genuine work of St. Francis.

7. Ibid.

8. Ibid.

9. Ibid.

10. Ibid.

11. Ibid.

12. St. Francis, *Letter to Anthony.*

13. Paul Gallico, "St. Francis and the Animals," in *Saints For Now,* ed. Clare Booth Luce (New York: Sheed and Ward, 1952), 121.

14. Constantine Koser, "St. Francis and Man," in *Our Life With God* (Pulaski, Wisc.: Franciscan Publishers, 1971), 142.

15. Henri Daniel-Rops, *Cathedral and Crusade,* trans. John Warrington (New York: Image, 1963), 2:254.

16. Ibid., 1:188.

17. Arthur Koestler, *Darkness at Noon,* trans. Daphne Hardy (New York: New American Library, 1955), 45.

Destiny

1. LM, 14.5.

2. St. Bonaventure, *Excerpts,* 28.

3. The authors understand very well that there are many other issues confronting the human family on the eve of the twenty-first century. This list is not intended to be definitive, but simply exploratory of the dimensions for ministry in the future.

4. St. Francis, *Letter to All the Faithful.*

5. Ibid.

6. 3S, 58.

7. St. Francis, *The Admonitions,* 15.

8. St. Francis, *The Rule of 1221,* 9.

9. The material and quotations for this section (including that of W. E. Gladstone) are found in Harry Emerson Fosdick, *Successful Christian Living: Sermons on Christianity Today* (New York: Harper & Row, 1937), 120–30.

10. 1C, 76.

11. St. Francis, *The Rule of 1223,* 5.

12. Test.

13. St. Francis, *The Admonitions,* 14.

14. Ibid., 24.

15. Test.

16. 1C, 17.

17. Ibid.

18. LM, 14.1.

Bibliographic Essay

1. 2C, 32.62.

Index